GHOST STORIES
of
MONTANA

Dan Asfar

LONE
PINE

Lone Pine Publishing International

The Publisher: Lone Pine Publishing International
Distributed by Lone Pine Publishing
1808 B Street NW, Suite 140
Auburn, WA 98001
USA

Websites: www.lonepinepublishing.com
www.ghostbooks.net

Publisher's Cataloging-In-Publication Data
(Prepared by The Donohue Group, Inc.)

Asfar, Dan, 1973-
  Ghost stories of Montana / Dan Asfar.

  p. : ill. ; cm.

  ISBN-13: 978-976-8200-36-5
  ISBN-10: 976-8200-36-7

1. Ghosts--Montana--Folklore. 2. Folklore--Montana. 3. Ghosts--Folklore.
4. Folklore--Montana. 5. Ghost stories. I. Title.

PZ8.1 .A84 2007
398.2/09/786/05

Photo Credits: Every effort has been made to accurately credit photographers. Any errors or omissions should be directed to the publisher for changes in future editions. The photographs in this book are reproduced with the kind permission of the following sources: Kate Leigh (p. 25); Library of Congress (p. 55: HABS MONT,2-CUST,1-1; p. 77: HAER MONT,47-BT.V,1D-3); Randy Mayes (p. 65); A. Plummer (p. 106); Ashok Rodrigues (p. 119); Laurin Johnson (p. 132); Mehmet Dilsiz (p. 159); Stuart Duncan (p. 169); Christopher Driscoll (p. 189).

The stories, folklore and legends in this book are based on the author's collection of sources including individuals whose experiences have led them to believe they have encountered phenomena of some kind or another. They are meant to entertain, and neither the publisher nor the author claims these stories represent fact.

For M.K. Fearney

Contents

Acknowledgments

It is with good cause that the non-fiction paranormal genre is generally greeted with its fair share of skepticism. Ever since the subject captured the general public's attention in the second half of the 19th century, there has been no shortage of hoaxes, charlatans and false prophets. Voices emerging from supposedly sound study and objective observation of purported supernatural phenomenon were uncovered as opportunists and fame seekers. And yet the genre persists, as old folktales continue to survive and new accounts of inexplicable phenomena emerge.

Every account in this volume is based on purported hauntings set in Montana. Some are old supernatural folktales retold, while others are based on interviews with individuals claiming to have come face to face with phenomena beyond their understanding. Still others are rooted in tales that have been unearthed by other authors in this genre.

Allow me to begin by acknowledging the invaluable contribution of those whose tales informed and inspired many of the stories in this book. Thanks to the individuals who took the time to share their strange experiences. The identities of these witnesses have been protected and given pseudonyms where they appear in the text.

Previous authors whose research has been invaluable to this text are eminent Montana paranormal researcher and raconteur, Debra D. Munn, author of *Big Sky Ghosts: Eerie True Tales of Montana,* Volume 1 (1993) and Volume 2 (1994), and Ellen Baumler, author of *Spirit Tailings:*

Ghost Tales From Virginia City, Butte and Helena (2002). Your work has done much to illuminate the paranormal remnants of that hardscrabble activity so often associated with Montana's history: mining. More than one story in this book was inspired and informed by your work.

Introduction

Montana—mythic, rugged and free—the last line of the American frontier, where ranchers, miners and farmers dug for profit next to the enduring Native American peoples. The last region of America's legendary unbridled West, the state was born from the hungry struggles of its first settlers—from the collision of individual ambition and the seemingly irresistible encroachment of the corporation. Yet even as ranchers and miners came under the shadow of big money, they owed much of their existence to the Eastern funding of the ever-expanding railroad and to the forays of the Federal army against defiant Native braves. The clash and clamor of these historic struggles define much of what makes up Montana culture today. While the state's wealth is owed to the striving of its first citizens, much of the landscape is littered with reminders of its often-brutal narrative. There are the abandoned towns strewn across the former mining sites, the battlefields, the discontinued rail lines, the deserted homesteads. And, of course, there are the ghosts.

Ghosts—whether you look within Billings, Great Falls or Missoula, New York, London, Hong Kong or Dublin, you will find stories of the past told through ghost stories. In the American Rockies or the bogs of Ireland, the streets of Helena or the alleys of New England, there are sure to be ghosts lurking upon the landscape. Or, maybe it would be more accurate to say, there are sure to be ghost stories. And there always have been.

As long as people have been putting pen to paper, there have been ghosts in popular storytelling. There are ghosts in Homer's *Iliad,* one of the original narratives of Western Civilization. Ghosts make numerous appearances in the plays of William Shakespeare. The storytellers of the 19th century had a seemingly insatiable appetite for ghosts in their fiction. From Charles Dickens to John Keats to Edgar Allan Poe, there is an overabundance of supernatural material. That's to say nothing of Victorian England's obsession with Spiritualism and the resulting gothic narratives that fueled the popular imagination and gave birth to the undying dead, the vampires of Bram Stoker and Frankenstein's creature to name the most well known. In the 20th century, the ongoing fascination has found voice in the seemingly endless popularity of writers like H.P. Lovecraft, Stephen King and Anne Rice. On screen, there are the armies of brain-eating corpses in countless zombie flicks and hundreds of horror movies featuring restless spirits of the dead.

One of the interesting things about the supernatural in entertainment, however, is how the notion of ghosts says something about who we are as a people. There's no arguing that the dead have always occupied a big place in cultural expression; the inevitability of death and the question of what follows forms one of the biggest questions, or perhaps, *the* biggest question regarding the human condition. Cultures near and far, remote and cosmopolitan can be partly understood by the way their religious beliefs and folkloric narratives tackle the notion of the great hereafter. What does this say about our contemporary culture, then, that the notion of ghosts is so widely accepted within entertainment, yet generally rejected in reality? If, as most level-headed Americans would likely state, there is no such thing as ghosts, then why do we continue to be so fascinated by them? In the end, ghost stories are so popular because whether we are prone to dwell upon it or not, death concerns us all.

No need to worry. The following pages do not attempt to tackle such questions. This is a book of ghost stories, nothing more, and it probably goes without saying that the reader didn't pick it up with hopes of coming to grips with such issues. Yet it must be stated that not one of the tales have hatched from the whimsy of the author's imagination. All of these stories are said to be true—supernatural accounts told by Montanans, ghostly folklore that has survived the centuries, some stories well known, others more obscure—each and every one of them is purported to find its roots in fact, rather than fiction. These are Montana's ghost stories; the author can only claim to be a faithful chronicler of some of the haunts in its history and the uncanny experiences of its citizens. It is up to the readers to decide whether or not to believe.

1
Haunted
Houses

The Ghost of
Judge Theodore Brantley

The town of Helena was born in the violent throes of gold fever, among a throng of fortune hunters who flooded into the area in 1864, when gold was discovered in Last Chance Gulch. During those early years, it was about as rough as any boomtown that blighted the frontier. A settlement of hastily constructed log cabins and pine plank boxes built by young men willing to do anything to make their fortunes, Helena was a lawless and frantic place.

Many frontier towns, like Helena, did not make it far. Zealous whiskey-fueled men who lived and died for a flash in the pan generally do not make for the healthiest, most lasting communities. As a rule, these frontier prospectors let almost nothing get in the way of their hunt for mineral wealth; they wore their justice in their holsters and usually did not hesitate in dispensing it when their neighbors' ambitions interfered with their own. Respectable women were rare in these ramshackle burgs, while families were even rarer. And when the gold or the silver ran out, the horde of fortune seekers left as quickly as they came, leaving a deserted husk behind.

This fate would not be Helena's, however. Many of the men who struck it rich developed a fondness for the beautiful town and settled there after the first rush subsided. They put down roots: built homes, started families, established schools and churches. Still, there were feral elements in town—the hard-drinking gamblers who clung to their bottles and their six-shooters, and the fiercely independent frontiersmen who refused to recognize anyone's rules but their own—and doubtless, they were a concern to those who valued law and order. The town of Helena was still growing after all, and there was no guarantee that it was going to develop into a respectable burg.

So when Judge Theodore Brantley came to town, he brought with him irrefutable assurances of civilization. From his starched collar to his stiff sense of propriety, Brantley was a living personification of Victorian morality. His arrival in town made it obvious to even the most depraved frontiersman eking out a dubious existence on the edge of town—the establishment had arrived, and it was here to stay.

The common narrative of the West has a fearless lawman, with steady hands and sure aim, riding in to establish proper law and order in the wild frontier town. This was not the case with Theodore Brantley, however. No six-shooter hung from his side; he did not make it his business to stare down drunken ne'er-do-wells. There were no legendary confrontations between him and the town's troublemakers.

With Brantley, it was his genteel manner—his unflappable, day-to-day behavior that was typical in the upper-class circles he came from back east—that eventually tamed the rough-and-tumble populace in Helena. Every morning, the judge walked with authority to his office, head up, chest out, always in his flawlessly tailored suit and towering stovepipe hat, greeting everyone he met formally in the streets.

He was not one to pontificate, but rather he believed in leading by example. To that end, he worked ceaselessly, his days governed by a severe self-discipline that gave him

During those early years, Helena was about as rough as any boomtown that blighted the frontier.

almost no time for leisure, or, for that matter, misbehavior. The old adage about idle hands and the Devil's work would have made Brantley into a saint of the work ethic. And, indeed, some might say he was industrious to a fault, spending most of his waking hours poring over legal documents and spending little time with his wife and children.

This is another fact about Brantley: he did not come to Helena alone. He brought his family, and he built one of the grandest homes in town for them to live in. Completed in 1887, the Brantley House was boldly perched over the town of Helena, a stately Victorian structure that seemed to issue a bold challenge to its wild surroundings, as though to say: this is the new order.

If Judge Brantley personified the approaching order that was on the verge winning the American West, then it might be said that his home was a natural extension of that order. The looming three-story mansion complete with oak accents and opulent furnishings was more than a mere home for Brantley and his family, it was a political edifice that represented his power and his commitment to Helena.

Theodore Brantley died in 1922, having lived long enough to see his vision come to be. By then, Helena was well past its humble frontier origins. Established as the capital of the burgeoning state, it was obvious by this time that the western Montana town was there to stay. As it turned out, so was the Brantley House. The Brantleys owned it for almost five decades after Theodore passed. One wonders if the venerable old judge would have been able to imagine what the future held, how far progress and industry would go and what his adopted hometown would come to look like.

In truth, it is probably unlikely that many people have lent such musings to the long-dead judge. As exceptional a man as he was, history has reduced him to a relatively minor character in the epic story of the American West, practically forgotten by all but a small number of historical enthusiasts. And yet he would not remain forgotten. Eventually, local folklore would resurrect him.

Or, *something* resurrected him, anyway. The popular version tells us that it all began when the Brantley family finally sold the judge's Holder Street house. It was 1970, shortly after the new owners had moved in and started renovating the historic house when the old judge began to get attention once again—or, at least, among those inclined to believe in ghosts anyway.

The first bizarre occurrence in the Brantley House took place a few weeks after the house changed hands. It was on an evening in the middle of the week when the couple were hard at work, beginning their renovations with a thorough gutting of the third floor, when the crash and bang of their work was suddenly interrupted by a louder noise from the ground floor—a heavy creaking sound they both instantly recognized as their front door. There was the sound of the door opening, followed by the swift and sudden sound of it slamming shut. The couple jumped, looked at one another, and then the sound of footsteps trudging up the ornate spiral staircase began. It sounded like a big man with heavy boots had entered their home. The footfalls did not flag or pause but took the stairs with a constant cadence, taking their time. Louder and louder they became, getting ever closer to the third floor.

The owners could only stand and stare as the footfalls plodded down the hallway. The inexplicable chill working up their backs kept them rooted there as whoever was in the hallway stopped in front of every door, opened it and then carried on to the next, falling silent only at the end of the passage. It was only then that the couple worked up the nerve to act, running out into the hall to see their guest. But there was no one there.

They did not believe it. Both had heard the exact same thing, so it was impossible that they had imagined it. And yet their eyes could not be lying either—there was no one in sight. Was it possible that their uninvited guest was heavy coming in but tiptoed his way down? If this was the case, the light-footed intruder was still in the house because neither of them had heard the front door creak back open. They conducted a thorough search of the entire house, but no one was there. Besides their three children and themselves, Brantley House was empty.

It was not the only time the mysterious footsteps toured the third floor. In fact, it became a semi-regular occurrence. The invisible visitor always arrived late in the night, sometime past 10 o'clock, and always on week-nights. His passage never varied. Entering through the front door, he trudged up the spiral staircase. Always with the same slow, heavy cadence, the sound of footsteps pause at the top of the stairs, followed by the walk down the hall—stopping at every door, opening it slowly. At the end of the hall, they simply fell silent. Not once were they ever heard going back the other way.

Never once did the Brantley House's residents get a glimpse of their invisible visitor, so it was unusual that none of them ever felt frightened or threatened by their nightly guest. Somehow, they were able to sense that their plodding visitor had no intention of harm. In fact, they all agreed that they felt a kind of security when the front door creaked open. There was a sense that the presence cared and was checking up on them, just to make sure that everything was okay.

The couple soon did a little research and came up with a theory that made sense of what they were feeling. They learned that Brantley House's original patriarch, Judge Theodore Brantley, was a diligent worker who spent most of his weekdays working late. Apparently, he was also a man of routine. Every night, it was the same. He came home from work and, first thing, headed straight for the third floor. Everyone would already be in bed, but this did not stop him from checking up on them, stopping at each room, opening the door and taking a quick look—just to make sure everything was okay. Bizarre as the theory was, it was based on a belief in ghosts and the assumption that the judge was such a worrisome fellow, and it was the only one they had. So it was that the legend of Theodore Brantley's ghost was born.

But why now? For over the 80 years that the Brantley family owned the house, there had not been any accounts of ghostly footsteps marching up the stairs and across the third floor. Why would the spirit of old Judge Brantley suddenly start going through the motions of his earthly days?

When the phenomena became well known among paranormal enthusiasts, speculation abounded. People who studied ghostly matters recognized that the owners of the Brantley House were not the first to experience supernatural phenomena during home renovations. In fact, major renovations to old homes have often brought dormant spirits out of the woodwork. A house well loved by a deceased former resident would often contain part of their energy or essence, and any radical changes to the house could quite possibly release that energy into the material plane, making it visible or observable to the human senses. Or perhaps the spirit was simply unhappy with the changes. Another theory hinged on the familial make-up of the new residents, which was identical to Theodore Brantley's—a married couple with three children. Perhaps this fact alone somehow roused the old judge from his mortal slumber.

Either way, once the old judge began his nightly trudges, he did not seem to be in any rush to return to eternal rest. In fact, he began to get more active. Not that his heavy stride got any lighter, but the weary and heavy footfalls began to venture into another part of the house. Several weeks into his nightly tour of the stairwell and hall, the judge began venturing into the attic as well.

The attic forays occurred much later in the evening than his walk down the hall. The steps were as slow and heavy as before, but this time the sound of pacing could be heard across the attic room above the master bedroom. The couple was woken by the creaking floorboards above them. The sound continued, back and forth tirelessly, with no end in sight.

At first, the couple had no idea what to do about Brantley's new routine. Unlike his march across the third floor, which always ceased when he reached the last room in the hall, there was no apparent end to the pacing in the attic. On and on he went, keeping them up for hours. Then they discovered the secret staircase. The rickety ascent up to the attic was hidden behind a false wall in the bedroom. It was the only way to get to the attic as well as the only way to silence the judge's restless pacing. Whenever he began, all they had to do was to begin climbing the stairs. They did not have to go all the way up; the pacing would stop the moment they touched the first stair.

There was a historical explanation for the footsteps in the attic as well. Because of Theodore Brantley's remarkable work ethic, he did much of his work in the attic, which he converted into a study. According to a Brantley family account, he was in the habit of spending late nights there, working into the small hours. Yet as celebrated as he was for his obsessive diligence to his work, his wife could not have been too happy about it, being kept awake by the preoccupied pacing as he wrangled with the legal issues of his day. Certainly, the new residents sleeping in the master bedroom could attest to how disturbing this habit must have been. Did the judge grow accustomed to the sound of his wife taking the stairs to tell him to quit his pacing, so that eventually the sound of her foot on the first step was enough for him to stop and sit down?

The above phenomena were easily explained by Theodore Brantley's routine, but there were some facets to the somber judge that might well have been unknown, had it not been for the behavior of his suddenly active ghost. Most notably, the new owners had reason to believe the Montana judge was afflicted by a potent sweet tooth.

The new residents had a basement tenant, who was in the habit of keeping a full candy dish in her kitchen, and her candy had a way of vanishing all on its own in the Brantley House. It turned out to be a costly habit; sometimes it was a gradual pilfering—a little here, a little there, taking a week or longer—before the tenant realized that she was not consuming the sweets as quickly as they were disappearing. On other occasions, it was a shocking event, when half the candy would vanish in the time it took for her to turn her back. More than once, the sugar-loving phantom swiped the entire dish just moments after she had filled it up.

These were not the only occurrences said to go on in the house. It appears as though the judge may have acquired a certain fascination for the amenities of the 20th century. On numerous occasions, the owners returned from family outings to find their house buzzing in electric cacophony, with practically every household appliance connected to an outlet in full operation: television and radios on full volume, blenders whirring, dishwasher running, even the electric shaver buzzing away in the bathroom. Fascinated as he was with these domestic implements, Judge Brantley was still conscious of his manners and always took care to switch everything off himself soon after the family opened the door. Everything in the house was running one moment and suddenly went dead the next. The owners were rattled only the first few times it happened. There was no question in their minds that it was curiosity, not maliciousness, that motivated their resident haunt.

So it was that the Brantley House's new owners found it relatively easy to accept the presence of the ghost. Regardless of what history knew about Theodore Brantley, they sensed, they just *knew*, that there was nothing malevolent about the spirit in their home. The couple ended up moving out when their kids went away for college, but to this day, residents have remained tolerant to the supposedly continuing ghostly goings-on. The judge, everyone knows, has no intention of doing anyone any harm. In fact, there is a sense that the reawakened spirit has assumed a sort of vigil over his former home. For those who did not mind the feeling of being watched by a protective eye, the ghost of Judge Brantley was actually a welcomed presence. For those who did not appreciate regular plundering of their store of candy bars and M&Ms, however, the ghost of Judge Brantley was probably more of a nuisance than anything else.

A Billings Haunting

"We've lived in Billings for quite some time," says this life-long Montana resident, who shall go by the pseudonym "Richard Carter" for the purpose of this story. "And there's been something up with our house for as long as anyone in our family can remember. I was too young to remember any of it when we moved in, but my mother says she knew that the place wasn't a normal house inside of a week."

Carter's mother did not tell him this outright. According to her son, she kept the strange goings-on from her kids for as long as possible because she worried they might milk the presence of a resident ghost for all it was worth—extending bed time for as long as possible, using it as an excuse to get out of having to do homework or chores. She denied it for as long as it was possible, having them believe that the hallway light on the second floor flickered in the middle of the night on account of a faulty circuit. She gave a similar explanation for the television, which had a tendency to switch on by itself. The black silhouette that occasionally appeared in their doorway in the middle of the night was their sleepwalking father, and the suddenly plummeting temperature in certain rooms was a faulty thermostat.

"It was years before she told us the story about how, on the first day we moved in, all the boxes they had stacked in the room that they were going to make into the home office flipped over upside down when my parents were in another room." Carter says that this room, the home office, would become the locus for much of the supernatural phenomena that occurred in the house.

"One of the things that used to happen a lot was the footsteps in the upstairs hall," Carter says. "I remember waking up every now and then to the sound of these footsteps clomping down the hall. They were always coming down the hall from the office. Sometimes my bedroom door would open, and I'd see this black shape, supposedly my sleepwalking dad, standing at the doorway before shutting the door and walking back to the office."

Although he and his siblings believed their mother for some time, Carter says that he always had nagging doubts about his mother's explanations. "The typical tendency, I think, is to assume kids are stupid," he says. "You know, parents can tell their kids anything and they'll buy it. Maybe that's partly true, but kids can be really observant."

One of the things that bothered Carter for a long time was how the figure that appeared at his doorway seemed significantly bigger than his father. "I'd call my dad a guy with a pretty average physique. There's nothing about him that really stands out, one way or the other." Yet the man who appeared at his doorway when he was young was taller and broader than his father, with a much slower and heavier footstep.

"I'm sure there was a time or two when I called my mom on it. You know, saying that this guy, he's not Dad, but when you're a certain age and your mom tells you something, you're likely going to believe her." So even though Carter had his doubts, his childhood faith in his mother's word carried him through.

"The thing with the TV could be hard to buy, too. Like there's no one anywhere near the remote and the TV switches on all by itself. I'd ask Mom about it, and she'd

Richard could hear footsteps clomping down the hall in the evenings.

tell me the remote was busted. 'Great,' I'm thinking, 'but there's nobody even *close* to the remote, right?'"

Unlike Carter's mother, his father was always quiet on the subject, never answering any of his son's queries about the goings-on. "I'd ask him about his sleepwalking every now and then, or about anything else that might have been going on, like the TV or the light in the hallway or whatever, and he'd never give me a straight answer. He'd always say something like, 'Go talk to your mom.'" Carter's mother would subsequently provide her son with a cover-up story.

While Carter's mother was certainly conscious of how the presence of a spirit in her home could feasibly make parenting more difficult, she could not be said to be negligent in the way she simply accepted the paranormal presence as part of her home. In short, she had reason to believe that the spirit was not harmful, but was rather a benign ghost that was happy to be living alongside the Carter family, even occasionally assisting them in some mundane duty. "It's out there to say, but my mom *liked* having him around. She said he made her feel safe, like he was watching over us."

Something approximating a relationship began to form soon after the Carters moved in. After the initial stunt where all the boxes in the office were rearranged upside down, the spirit actually seemed to be helping them settle in. "My mom's got stories of coming home one day and finding all the plates she just pulled out of a box stacked up neat in the cupboard. Once or twice early on, she went downstairs to grab the laundry out of the dryer and all the clothes were already piled into the hamper. Little things like that," Carter says.

But most importantly, the mysterious presence was protective of her children. "Mom has this story where we just moved in and I was crawling around on the kitchen floor. Dad had been doing some kind of renovating in there, and there were a bunch of nails on the floor. My mom says she walked in just in time to see a whole bag of nails rolling away from me, all on their own. I was reaching out, trying to grab them, but they rolled right over to my mom's feet." Carter continues: "There's also this story my mom tells about how when I was one or so, I'd escaped from my crib and started crawling down the hall. My parents had company over, but when my mom heard these three knocks from the office upstairs, she went to investigate right away. She was just in time to see me at the top of the stairs, taking the first step down. She always says that if she had arrived a few seconds later, I would have fallen down the stairs."

Occurrences like this convinced Carter's mother that whatever was residing in their home had her family's best interests at heart, despite the eeriness of the footsteps in the hall or the watchful silhouette at her children's doorways. Her husband, however, was far less thrilled about the ghostly presence. "They never talked about it directly in front of us, but it was pretty obvious that my dad wasn't happy that this stuff was going on in our place. There was always this tension between my mom and dad about it. We learned after a while not to talk about it in front of him. He never shouted about it or anything. Things would just get quiet and uncomfortable."

His parents never openly discussed the issue with them, but Carter formulated a theory. His mother, essentially pragmatic by nature, was quickly able to look past the inherent creepiness of their invisible housemate and accept him as an extra pair of helping hands. "It sounds weird, I know, but I really think that my mom didn't give too much thought to who he was or why he was there. She had a lot on her plate, and once she got used to the idea that our place was haunted, she was just happy to use it to her advantage."

Carter's father, however, was not nearly so comfortable with the situation. "Yeah, I don't know what to say about that for sure, just that Dad obviously had issues with it. He never said much to us, but it was pretty obvious that he felt like the odd man out. My mom was always looking on the bright side whenever the light in the hall would flicker on and off or when the temperature in the office would plummet, but my dad didn't have the same attitude at all. He would get really bothered by it all. He had real problems with the situation."

Carter says that because he never really had a conversation with his father regarding their spectral housemate, all he is able to offer is speculation. "On some level, I think my dad refused to acknowledge that there was somebody else there. It was his way of coping with the idea that there was this other man watching over his kids and wife. I can't really blame him. I don't think there are a lot of people who would be too thrilled, actually." But then Carter goes on to say that the problem did not lie solely with his father. For as much as his father was adverse to sharing his house with the incorporeal presence, so too did this spirit seem unhappy with the fact that there was a man of the house.

Carter goes on to describe the weird competitive energy that existed between his father and the spirit: "There were all sorts of little things. Like sometimes we'd all be eating dinner. We were all be fine; nothing out of the ordinary was going on at all, but Dad would start complaining about how cold it was, which was crazy because all the rest of us were fine. Sometimes it would be warm enough for T-shirts, and there was Dad with a sweater on, not happy at all."

The intermittent chill that settled on his father was not confined to the dinner table; it would follow him around the house and would not dissipate until his father stepped out of the house. "It happened mostly when the whole family was together in one room," Carter says. "Dad would have to go up and put on extra layers or else leave the house for a few minutes. He didn't talk about it too much, but he wasn't happy about it, either. I remember he'd go quiet or else get all moody." Such ongoing occurrences would eventually become an issue between Carter's parents. "'Cause I was so young, I wasn't sure what was happening back then. They have had their problems like any other married couple," Carter says. "But I'm sure that this was a reason for one of their major differences."

Always his mother's son, Carter admits that when he was a child, his sympathies tended to be with his mother, while acknowledging today that the conditions must have been difficult for his father. "Imagine it—always feeling that low-key hostility, like you were never welcome in your own home, while hanging out with your own family. When I think about it now, I'm pretty amazed at how well he dealt with it."

It was a difficult situation that must have gotten more difficult as the rest of the family grew closer with the mostly benevolent presence in their house. "By five or six years old, we were old enough to accept that it wasn't Dad pacing up and down the hallway. Even then, none of us were spooked by it. He'd been around forever, and we were used to him by then. We all had Mom's attitude, I think—like it was nice to have him around." Carter takes the credit for giving him his name. "I started calling him Oscar, after Oscar the Grouch, and it stuck."

Despite his namesake, Oscar did not exhibit any excessively grouchy behavior. He was not such a big fan of Carter's father, but Oscar had a way of doting over the children. Or that's the way that Carter chose to interpret the footsteps in the hall and the check-ups at his doorway. "For sure most people won't get how a guy could be so okay about living with a ghost and not be even a little scared about it," Carter says. "For us, though, growing up with Oscar, it's something we got used to. I always had this kind of vague knowledge that having Oscar with us wasn't normal, but it didn't bother me too much. As a kid, you learn the rules quick enough."

When Carter says "the rules," he means what is and what is not acceptable in the outside world—in his case, what he could and could not talk about in school. "Most people aren't sure how to take a kid who talks about how he lives with a friendly invisible man named Oscar. It was a lesson I learned as early as the first grade: don't tell your classmates about Oscar. They won't get it."

Not that Oscar remained foremost in Carter's mind for too long. The household ghost's fate paralleled that of other children's countless imaginary friends—Oscar's presence began to fade as Carter and his siblings became more immersed in the world outside of their house. "I don't really have a clear memory of how it happened," Carter says today. "I don't think it was abrupt—like he was stomping up and down that hallway every night and then one day he just stopped. I think it took, maybe, years. It was so gradual that we barely even noticed that it happened."

There is a trace of sadness in Carter's account of Oscar's withdrawal. "It's funny that I never thought about it for years," he says, "but years went by with almost nothing weird happening, and it never occurred to me to wonder where he'd gone to. I don't think I ever went up to my mom and asked her, 'What happened to Oscar?' Sometimes I wonder if we were the ones who drove him away. Kids he didn't know started coming over to the house. We were having sleepovers. I think he knew that we didn't really need him to be so protective." This is just a theory, but Carter admits to being somewhat nostalgic when he thinks about his childhood haunt.

Oscar didn't vanish all together. "He wasn't showing up as much as he used to, but I don't think he ever left for good," Carter says. "Little things would happen every now and then. Like once or twice a year, a load of clothes would be taken out of the dryer on their own. The television would still switch on by itself from time to time, and Mom was always happy when Oscar would do those little things, like move dirty dishes into the sink when no one was in the kitchen. Once, I'd forgotten my keys at home when I went to school, and I would have been locked out of the house until my parents got home. But when I got home, the keys were behind the screen door. I asked my parents about it, but neither of them had put the keys out. We left it alone after that, but I'm sure we were all thinking the same thing: it was Oscar.

"There was also the time in high school, years and years later, when my sister broke up with her first serious boyfriend," Carter continues. "It was really glum at our place for a week or two. Her room is the next one over from mine, and I remember the night I could hear her crying low in bed. A little while later, I heard footsteps in the hallway. I hadn't heard them for years and years, but I knew that Oscar was out there again, worried about my sister."

Carter maintains that Oscar occasionally returned to help out, but he also came back every now and then to irritate Carter's father. "It didn't happen nearly as much as it used to, but once in a while you'd see my dad in a very foul mood and know that Oscar had been fooling with him again. Of all the things Oscar did that irritated my dad, probably the worst was the way he fooled around with the lights in the hall. Well, it didn't happen too much, and Dad had to be happy about that, but his office upstairs would still get awfully cold. I've walked in on him a few times in the middle of summer and seen him in there doing his work with a sweater, shirt and pants on—in the middle of a heat wave."

Nostalgic as Carter is about growing up with a friendly ghost, Oscar seems to have almost moved on. Moved on to where, though, Carter can only guess. "I don't usually sit around thinking about the past," he says. "A few times, though, it's hit me how little any of us knew about Oscar. Really, why was he in our house in the first place? Why was he so protective over us kids? Why did he help out Mom and make Dad feel like he was a visitor in his own home?"

Carter says he admires his parents for how easily they were able to adapt to Oscar's presence. "Because if you think about it, something like that could really put a strain on a family. It would get tense sometimes, but we kids didn't get much of that at all." Yet at the same time, Carter expresses regret that no one ever tried to find out anything about Oscar. That kind of active curiosity had no place where their friendly ghost was concerned. "I don't know what their reasons were, exactly, but my parents never talked much about Oscar. Mom talked about him just a few times when we were small, but never when Dad was around. And Dad would get angry about the whole thing, but he never, never, said a word about him. They were super strange about it."

Today, Carter suspects that his parents knew something about Oscar that they were not telling. He says he would approach them about it now, but he would feel strange about asking such questions—partly because it has been so long and partly because the topic had always been so obviously off limits.

Then some of his mother's pragmatism comes out in him: "And why?" he asks. Whatever issues he detected between his parents when he was growing up, and however Oscar's presence factored into them, they were no longer relevant. "I don't see my parents as much as I used to, but they're fine now. Why would I want to bring up this uncomfortable past, especially when it doesn't matter anymore?"

Two Haunted Helena Houses

The Tatem House

The B.H. Tatem House stands out among the grand Victorian homes that line the streets of Helena's upper-west side. With its Tudor-era beam work and gothic windows, there is a distinct medieval feel to the imposing and beautiful edifice. It is adorned by architectural styles that predate many of the surrounding 19th-century homes, creating a sense of timelessness and authority. It's fitting then, that the mansion defies efforts to pin an exact date of construction upon it. One of the problems lies in the foundation. Apparently not built for the mansion that stands upon it now, the foundation does not seem to be made of rock from the local quarries. Also, local historians have had difficulty finding documentation for an exact construction date.

Of course, this is not to say that there is no history whatsoever on the house, or that it has *always* been there. It was constructed by one Benjamin H. Tatem, who arrived in Helena in 1870, working to manage the Columbia Mining Company's Unionville claims. An opportunist and entrepreneur, Tatem managed to make the most of his time in Helena. He took up the operation of one of the town's early iron foundries, while also earning himself a tidy profit on gold mine claims in Marysville. Rising to become one of the town's most prosperous members, he also kept close ties with Washington, winning his cushy appointment as U.S. Assayer from President James McKinley in 1901.

By that time, he was already living in his historic mansion, which was built, it has been estimated, sometime around 1893. He lived on among Helena's elite until 1915, leaving his lively and gregarious widow to manage his estate. Mrs. Tatem was 82 years old, but still in good health in 1922, when she met her sudden end on the corner of Lawrence Street and Benton Avenue, hit by a street trolley as she was crossing the street.

By all accounts, Mrs. Tatem had been a most gracious and generous host, but it seems as though two things haunted her: a driving compulsion to keep her mansion spotless and a deep-seated fear of burglars. Her housekeepers were freed of their duties when the matron passed on, but signs of her obsessive protection against theft remained evident for years to come. Hoping to keep her possessions safe from theft in the event of a break-in, Mrs. Tatem hid away her best dinnerware in random places all over her house. For years, subsequent residents of the old mansion would find little treasures in unlikely places all over the house—reminders of the over-protective matron who once resided there.

But these were not the only reminders. Other, far more unsettling discoveries have been reported from time to time. The years have brought accounts of all sorts of strange sounds. Some people have spoken of disembodied footsteps up and down the stairs of the house. At other times, witnesses have spoken of distant voices conversing on the upper floor, when there was no one there. Also, Mrs. Tatem's housekeepers have been known to return from time to time, with the sound of their knees and their brushes moving tirelessly over the hardwood floor.

The Ghost at 600 Harrison

Benjamin Tatem was not the only man who struck it rich in Helena. Indeed, there was a time when the state's capital was one of the richest cities in the country, its streets lined with the wealth of its mines, railways, ranches and lumber. The stately homes of its upper west side are what remain of that prosperous era—monuments to the fortune the most ambitious, ruthless and well-connected strivers were able to amass.

Thomas C. Power was one of these strivers. A first-generation American of Irish lineage, he made his first trip West when he was 21 years old, leaving his Iowa home to join a federal surveying party at the onset of the Civil War. By 1867, he was at Fort Benton. There he began his life-long entrepreneurial career, which would take him from running somewhere in the number of 100 companies, from freighting down the Missouri River to mining, ranching, banking and eventually politics, going as far as one term in the United States Senate. It was 1889 when, taking his place as one of Helena's undeniable elite, he had his mansion built.

By all accounts, he and his wife, Mary Flanagan, made the most of their wealth, throwing sumptuous parties for friends and acquaintances and becoming the center of Helena high society. Their son, Charles, inherited the house after they passed, and when his time came, he deeded the mansion to the Catholic Church. Under the Church's supervision, the mansion became a convent and a rectory, home to nuns, bishops and caretakers. It was the latter group who emerged with the accounts of the strange goings-on.

According to some of these church employees, frequent inexplicable phenomena had convinced them that something strange was afoot at the old manse. Caretakers spoke of lights flickering on and off for no apparent reason, footsteps in the upstairs hall, noises in the main floor foyer and a racket on the top floor. They are always at night, always when they were settling down for bed. While no one has ever claimed to *see* anything, the most common theories generally involve the spirit of a deceased maid, onetime resident Bishop Gilmore or the founder of the house, Thomas Power.

Although no one can decide on who the spirit is, there is a common point with most of the accounts: the furniture. One caretaker speaks of how he was informed that his bedroom contained all original furnishings from the 19th century, and that his bed was the same bed that Power himself slept and eventually died in. Not at all bothered by this fact, the man was still profoundly disturbed by the things that were going on while he worked there—the lights, the footsteps and, especially, the noises upstairs.

More than once, this caretaker contended with a mysterious party going on in the ballroom. Woken at night by the sound of music, laughter and conversation coming from the big room on the top-floor, the caretaker was most frightened the first time he heard it, unsure whether or not he had the nerve to get out of bed and investigate. Finally steeling himself for the experience, he rose and took to the stairs. The voluble good cheer became louder, more distinct, as the frightened caretaker made his way through the darkness of the house. Individual voices emerged from the buzz of conversation; the music was clear and there was the clink of glasses. By the time the caretaker made it to the ballroom entrance, he was entirely convinced that he would find a grand fête in full swing upon opening the door. But the moment he opened the door, the sound within died instantly. The ballroom was dark and empty. No one was there.

He was not the only caretaker to deal with the bizarre goings-on in the house. Another employee of the archdiocese was awoken to the sound of someone in the main floor foyer. His first thought being that someone had broken in and was trying to make away with valuables downstairs, so this man did not waste any time leaping from his bed and running down to confront the intruder. But there was no one there. And the moment he jumped off the last step, the noises in the foyer stopped.

There was no trace of anyone having been there, either. It was while he was looking through the main floor to make sure that nothing had been stolen that he noticed the portrait of Bishop Gilmore. He had seen it many times before, but there was something about the painting that night, a life that shone from it that had not been there before. Then he glanced at the formal chair situated in the foyer, which had belonged to the bishop while he was alive. In that instant, the caretaker was certain that the bishop was sitting there, looking back at him. He could not *see* anyone there, but he was certain nonetheless—the spirit of the bishop was *there*.

The church would eventually sell Power's mansion, and it was made into a day care. To this day, the occasional parent picking up his or her child will sense that something is not quite right in the ballroom—there are the faintest strains of music and the weird feeling of being surrounded by a room full of dancers. Could it be that old guests of the Powers' enjoyed the parties there so much that they have decided to say on? Or is it some sort of psychic residue of parties gone by? Who these dancers are, and why they have chosen to continue their supernatural festivities in this Helena mansion, is anyone's guess.

Guests in a Haunted House

"Mary Walters" is the pseudonym of a woman who states that she still lives in Montana, but, in the interests of maintaining her anonymity, does not say where. "We used to live in Great Falls, but most of the rest of the family was down in Billings back then, so we spent a lot of time there—holidays, every second or third weekend," she says. "Our family was close in those days, and it was always great fun to visit. All of us kids were about the same age and it was always a big deal whenever we made the trip." She says her family in Billings was composed of three households of uncles, aunts and cousins, but most of the family's loud reunions took place in just one of the homes. "My dad's eldest brother had the biggest house," she says. "It was a creaky old place, and he lived there with my aunt and three of my cousins." It was in this house that Walters claims to have had the inexplicable experiences that have remained with her over the years.

"For as long as I can remember, something about that house was weird, spooky and magical. I don't think I ever really knew what to make of it. I mean, I remember being scared and excited about it at the same time. Even before things started getting out of hand, there was a feeling in that house I'll never forget." The feeling was as capricious as it was powerful, sometimes leaving her anxious and other times filling her with an inexplicable thrill. "When I was between 9 and 10, I remember getting that weird charge every time we made the trip down to Billings. There was a mystery to the place that I was tuned into."

Walters is not sure how to explain the specific nature of this "mystery," but speaks of the way the house seemed to have a personality, even an intelligence. She talks about the way its creaks punctuated the weight of nighttime silences, and the tint of shadowy corners. "I suppose what was mysterious about the house was that it felt like it was way more than just a house, but I couldn't really say *why*."

The house sounds as though it might well be the generic haunted house presented in film and literature. It was old and lofty, with creaking floorboards, darkened halls and loose shutters. Mary Walters does not rule out the idea that the sight of the house might have been enough to inspire her early feelings of trepidation. "It couldn't have looked any more haunted, that's for sure," she says. "I think early on I liked the excitement that came with the fear. If you asked me when I was nine to go down into that basement alone, I wouldn't have done it for all the chocolate ice cream in the world." Nevertheless, Walters goes on to explain that there was some part of her that enjoyed the fact that she was so frightened by the house. It added another level of excitement to the family visits.

"My cousins definitely clued into the same thing," she says. "They had a stable of stories going from day one. They didn't waste much time telling them whenever we got together, either. There was the story about the white lady who lived in the attic and walked down into the basement every night. Then there was a hanging corpse in the guest bedroom that would show up at night, untie itself from the rafters and ask for a neck brace." Walters' cousins did not stop there. They told of a pale apparition that routinely appeared in the kitchen, ran the water and put the oven on, then screamed at anyone who dared to interrupt this nocturnal food preparation. One of her girl cousins had apparently won the trust of a phantom cat that came out of her closet at night and curled up in her bed. The cousins described the image of a young girl who was frequently spotted sitting in an armchair in the living room. In short, the stately old house was teeming with supernatural entities.

Today, Walters believes these stories were rooted in her cousins' rambunctious imaginations. That said, she also says that she does not believe they were pure invention, but were inspired by real events. "I'm sure my first impressions of the house came from those stories," she says. "You could say they were fun, in the way a good scare can be fun." The tales whispered among her cousins seemed real enough to keep her awake for an hour or so after bedtime, but Walters never really believed them. "I got scared enough a few times to ask my mom about the stories, and I took it to heart when she told me that there was no such thing as ghosts."

As certain as she was of her mother's words, Walters was unable to shed her fear of the place and the stories her cousins told. But it was not until a prolonged stay over the Christmas holidays one year that Walters experienced a number of events that called her mother's assurances into question. "I remember that it was cold that Christmas, and the snow was piled high. We were down in Billings for a week or so over the holidays, and the house was full the whole time—about as frantic as you'd expect."

Eventful as the festive days were, it was what happened during the nights that stuck with Walters. "It was a long time ago; there's a lot about that Christmas that's hazy," she says. "I can't remember how long we were there when everything started happening. I can't remember what time it was when I started hearing those noises, and I can't remember where my cousins were when it all started, either." What she *does* remember is that she first heard footsteps treading through house sometime late at night, well after everyone had gone to bed, and that she seemed to be the only one who heard the steps.

"I was sleeping on a mattress on the floor in my cousin's room, and I could hear them clearly on the other side of the door," Walters says. "It sounded like something heavy dragging across the hall." She went to her cousin's bed and shook her awake. "By the time she was awake, though, the dragging stopped," continues Walters. "She didn't believe me either. The stories were one thing, but she wasn't happy about being woken up because her crazy little cousin heard something in the hall. The next morning, she didn't say a word about it. For all I knew, she didn't even remember that it happened."

Walters did not say anything either. She explains that she was never among the more extroverted of her cousins, so she did not relish the attention such a claim would surely bring. Furthermore, at that point, she was not certain about what she thought she had heard. Could it have been a dream, after all?

The answer came later that night, when she was woken again by the same sound. For many years to come, Walters remembered what she saw that night and would ever after try to determine what she saw when she opened the bedroom door. "The sound got louder when I opened the door. There was nobody in the hall, but the light hanging in the stairwell was on, and I could see a shadow on the hallway wall." It was the shadow of a person, a man, going slowly down the stairs. Other than her assumption that this presence was a man, the only other detail Walters was able to absorb was the smell. "No one in the house smoked cigars, but as soon as I opened that door, there was a real thick cigar smoke smell."

A frightened Walters shouted into the hall, asking who was there. There was no response, and when she called again, the light went out on its own, the shadow vanished and her mother stepped out of the next bedroom. "That was all. My mom quieted me down quick enough. I told her there was someone in the house, and she told me that I had a bad dream." Even then, Walters might have been inclined to believe her; there was not even a trace of the cigar smoke in the air.

Walters cannot recall exactly what happened the next day. She doesn't remember whether she talked at all about what she had seen, if she made a big fuss about the previous two nights, or if she kept her fear bottled up. Whatever the case, the adults decided that she was not comfortable in her cousin's room and that her fitful sleeps and strange dreams probably had something to do with her discomfort. That night she was moved downstairs to the foldout couch in the living room.

"I know I was scared about what was going on," Walters says today, "but I can't remember exactly *how* scared. I don't think I was completely crazy scared, because if I had been, I don't think they'd have been able to get me to stay down there so easily. By that point, I think I was sure something really weird was going on, but maybe I was equal parts scared and curious."

So if she had put up any kind of fight at being relocated to the living room, it was by no means a staunch one. As darkness fell over Billings that night, she waited anxiously beneath the bedcovers in the living room. "The Christmas tree lights were on and I'm pretty sure I fell asleep reading by those lights. When I woke up, there were footsteps coming down the stairs and the light in the stairwell was back on."

Rather than shout for help again, Walters remained tight-lipped and hid beneath her blanket, only peeking out to the stairway as the shadow of the man came slowly into sight. "A lot of the details about what happened are fuzzy now," she says, "but I still remember what I saw that night like it just happened. I saw him, this man, make it down to the bottom of the stairs. The only reason I knew he was a man was because of the shape of his head and his big shoulders. He looked really big standing next to the banister. But the light went out as soon as he was on the main floor, and he wasn't facing me, so I couldn't see any details."

There was enough light, however, to see that the mysterious intruder was walking and that he was moving away down the hall toward the kitchen. Walters could also see that the figure was walking with a heavy limp. The black silhouette lurched as it went, dragging a dead foot behind it. Somehow, at that moment, the young girl gathered her courage to go after it.

"I think I followed him because he didn't know I was there," Walters says. "Looking at him, I got this feeling that he was 'on automatic,' in a way—he didn't even know where he was or what he was doing, like he was going down those stairs because he didn't know what else to do with himself." Whatever this figure was, Walters was

"I'll never know if he saw me or if it was his habit to look down the hall before he went downstairs."

certain that it was some sort of non-sentient entity, dering dead through the house.

As the mysterious, limping presence continued to move toward the kitchen, Walters was more than a little frightened as she made her way down the hallway after it. "I've thought before about how crazy I was to decide it was a good idea to follow him, but the rooms in that house were full of family. Besides, this guy had a way of disappearing when I woke someone up."

So it was that Walters followed the big figure as it lumbered into the kitchen, staying on her toes and keeping her distance. "I smelled the cigar smoke again when I was in the hall between the kitchen and the stairs. I could see him in the kitchen, turning real slow to open the door that went down to the basement."

Still moving at its plodding pace, it was just about to walk through the doorway to the basement when it turned and looked straight at Walters. "I'll never know if he saw me or if it was his habit to look down the hall before he went downstairs," she says. "I know that I didn't see any part of a face. No nose, mouth or eyes. He was just a black shape, and he looked like that for a few seconds and then went down the stairs. The door shut by itself behind him."

At this point, Walters drew the line. She says she did not follow the black shape down the stairs, but slowly opened the door and looked into the basement. It was so dark, but she swears she was able to see the heavy shape descending clumsily. The pungent cigar smoke still wafted in the air, but it grew fainter and fainter. And the footsteps seemed to fade with each step. And then she was standing in the kitchen by herself—no footsteps, and not even a hint of cigar smoke. She waited there a while longer, half-expecting to hear shouting from her cousins who were downstairs. But there was only silence. Given her family's reactions from the previous two nights, Walters thought it was best not to tell anyone of what she had just seen. Instead, she went to back to her bed in the living room, sure that that she had seen a ghost. She is still sure today.

This unnerving nocturnal experience wasn't the only time she was aware of the presence in her cousins' home. "A few days after that, I was back upstairs sleeping on the floor in my cousin's room and I heard the dragging noise in the hall again. I didn't bother opening the door that time around. I let my cousin sleep and let the big dark entity go down to the basement in peace. He didn't seem to be doing any harm down there, anyway."

Over those holidays in that house, Mary Walters says she became aware of all sorts of strange little incidents that she had previously not been aware of. "Every time I went to bed, my nighttime book was in a different place. My dad kept complaining about how he was misplacing his cigarettes. I remember hearing the grown-ups talking about how bottles of wine and rum went missing. And the two cousins who were sleeping downstairs in the basement talked about having nightmares and weird dreams every night." All these events came with easy explanations, but with each case Walters found herself thinking about the ghostly black figure making its nightly tour from the top floor of the house to the bottom.

"I've carried what I saw in that house for the rest of my life. I wouldn't call myself obsessed about it, but I definitely got interested in spirits and ghosts, and I still read about all that stuff like mad."

Did she ever see the black figure again? "I never knew who he was and what he wanted there," is her reply. "We kept visiting for a few years, and I'd hear those footsteps some nights and smell that cigar, too. But after I saw him go down to the basement that one time, I left him alone. He wasn't doing anyone any harm, and I think I felt a bit sorry for him, creeping through that house alone at night for who knows how many years. I don't think he wanted to be bothered."

By the time Walters was 14, her uncle had sold the house and moved with his family elsewhere. She never visited it again. "I'm not called on to go to Billings so much anymore," Walters says, "but whenever I do find myself back in town, I always think about that man I saw on Christmas all those years back, and I wonder if he's still going down the stairs of that house."

2
Little
Bighorn

The Ghosts of Little Bighorn

The oldest building in Big Horn County can be found on the Crow Indian Reservation, looking out over a carefully manicured field of nearly 5000 dead and buried American soldiers. It is known simply as the Stone House. Two stories tall, aged gray and severe, it has stood for over 100 years next to the lonely graves of the Custer National Cemetery, a silent sentinel to a desolate and legendary landscape of death.

The Stone House was constructed in 1894, providing a lonely home for the cemetery caretaker. It was part of this man's not-so-cheery job to live in the house with incoming corpses that were kept downstairs before being laid to rest in the cemetery. Given the long list of bizarre occurrences that have been reported in this building over the years, however, it would seem that these cemetery caretakers often lived with unexpected residents. Indeed, it would seem that many of the bodies that have passed through the Stone House seemed to prefer the caretaker's company to the cold ground of the graveyard beyond.

The Stone House has served different purposes over the years. Originally a home for the cemetery caretaker, it was then turned into a summer residence for park employees, until, quite recently, being converted to the White Swan Memorial Library and the park historian's office. Most of the surviving accounts of the inexplicable goings-on took place in the mid-to-late 1980s, when the house was used primarily for employee lodging. Open only for the summers during this time, it was routinely locked up for the long winter months—which was purportedly when the ghosts emerged.

One of the more circulated accounts was originally narrated by Bob Reece in his oft-cited paper, "Visitors of Another Kind," which he presented to the Boulder Country Corral of Westerners in October 1990. The incident occurred one night during the spring of 1980, when a park employee, a historian named Mardell Plainfeather, was returning with her daughter to the employee apartments after a family visit. She was making her way to her suite when she saw that a light glowing from one of the windows on the Stone House's second floor. It was late spring, and Mardell knew that there were maintenance crews working there during the days, readying the place for the summer employees. Still, she had also heard the numerous stories about the Stone House and found herself struggling with a growing apprehension as she looked on at the illuminated window.

She did not want to venture into the house on her own, so she dropped in on her two friends and fellow workers, Mike and Ruth Massie, a married couple who lived in one of the other employee suites. Admitting that she felt skittish about checking the house alone, Plainfeather asked Mike if he would mind coming with her to turn off the light. When Mike saw Plainfeather's daughter in her arms, he told her to call it a night; he would go up on his own.

Mike pulled on his shoes and told his wife that he was stepping out to the Stone House to turn off a light on the second floor. Having no reason to be particularly interested, Ruth kept on watching television as her husband walked up to the house. The repetitive sound of dialogue and laugh track occupied the next several minutes and then the television went silent, and a cold feeling settled over Ruth Massie. A moment later, a heavy voice came from her TV speakers. It said two words: "Second floor."

Suddenly all she could think of was her husband up at the Stone House, switching off a light on the second floor. Like everyone else working at the battlefield, she also knew of the stories circulating about the building. Ruth ran to the house, waving at the windows in the hope that he would see her, all the while not sure what good this would accomplish.

Mike saw Ruth from the window after he switched off the light. No one had been inside when he entered, and pushing all the stories about sounds and apparitions out of his mind, he climbed the stairs and flicked off the switch. Nothing out of the ordinary had occurred, until, that is, he ran into his breathless wife halfway back to the apartment. Mike listened to her story, but he was not able to account for her concern. Nothing had happened. When they returned to the apartment, the television was still on and was working fine, back to the cadence of dialogue and laughter. And so it was that another strange chapter was added to the ongoing account of events at the Stone House.

Indeed, if the talking television was an isolated incident, the affair might easily be overlooked. It had been getting late, after all; it was certainly possible that Ruth had momentarily fallen asleep and dreamed that the voice was coming from her television set. Yet given the Stone House's long past of scaring employees, there was a general tendency for people from the park to take Ruth Massie's experience seriously. It is not the strangest thing said to have occurred within those walls.

The battlefield ranger who was woken in the middle of the night by a figure sitting at the edge of his bed would certainly have to agree. Coming out of sleep, he assumed for a moment that it was his wife, until he realized that she was visiting family, and he had gone to sleep by himself that night in the bedroom on the second floor. A rush of fear came with his realization, and the ranger lunged for the night table, where he kept his revolver. When he came back to the figure, it had left his bed and began floating chaotically around the room. He saw it clearly, then, by the moonlight through his window. The figure was floating because it had no legs—in fact it had no anchor to the ground whatsoever. It was a disembodied torso, without legs and without a head, moving blindly through his room. The ranger did not fire a single shot, but looked on speechless and in horror, as it finally found the doorway and made its departure.

Other apparitions have been sighted. When Stone House was divided into employee living quarters, numerous residents claimed to see a vaguely female figure drifting down the stairs; others spoke of seeing a lone army officer in archaic cavalry uniform staring down from the solitary circular window in the attic. Then there was Dan Martinez's experience in the summer of 1982, as presented by Debra Munn in her seminal work on Montana folklore, *Big Sky Ghosts: Eerie True Tales of Montana*, Volume 1 (1993).

Working at the Little Bighorn Battlefield ranger and interpreter during the summers from 1979 to 1985, Martinez confesses that he was in the habit of capitalizing on the Stone House's reputation. "I admit that when I was a seasonal there, I used to make up scary stories about the

Stone House, Little Bighorn Battlefield National Monument

Stone House so that other people would be afraid of it," he says to Ms. Munn. "That way, I could be sure of staying in the old place myself. I really enjoyed my time there and I never believed in such things as ghosts."

That was before his experience one night in June of 1982, when, waking from sleep in the top-floor room, he found himself staring up at an Indian brave looming over his bedside. Munn presents Martinez's testimony:

It was a moonlit night and I saw without a doubt that this person was an Indian, and he was just standing there staring down at me. I was absolutely powerless to move or to wake my wife lying beside me. I couldn't even speak as I watched this man. At first I thought he was a real person, because he looked absolutely solid and was dressed in all the trappings of an American

Indian. Most notable was an eagle feather hanging off to one side of his head. I could barely breathe and I felt as if there were a huge depression on my chest.

Lying there in bed, Martinez was literally paralyzed by the sight of his nocturnal visitor. His heart was racing and the sheets were soaking with his sweat, but Martinez was unable to move so much as his head. It was a very real and mortal terror that seized Martinez as he looked up at the Indian man's hard and merciless stare—a numbing terror that seemed to last an eternity, but, in actuality, could not have lasted any longer than a minute or two. In utter silence the man finally turned and strode out of the bedroom. "I was just frozen with terror and it took me a while before I was able to wake up my wife," Martinez says. The park historian concludes that while he cannot say for certain whether what he experienced was "dream or reality," it had a profound effect on him. Certainly, he stopped making up stories about ghosts in the historic house after that.

Supernatural activity in the Stone House is not limited to ghostly sightings. There have been disembodied footsteps and banging sounds coming from the walls of empty rooms. In other instances, heavy noises come from other vacant rooms, as though pieces of invisible furniture were being dragged across the floor by invisible movers. The number of baffling phenomena reported from the Stone House has led paranormal enthusiasts to claim that it might be the most haunted place in the state. Perhaps a better way to say it is that Stone House is located at the center of the most haunted site in the state. It is widely believed that there are restless spirits all over the Little Bighorn Battlefield.

Every year, an estimated 400,000 visitors come from near and far to walk the bloodied hill where the legendary lieutenant colonel and his Seventh Cavalry made their last stand. Guided by hubris, ambition, plain stupidity and no small amount of courage, 272 United States soldiers were brutally killed on the battlefield by an angry and merciless war party of the Sioux and Cheyenne.

It is not necessary to get into the details of the battle here. Those readers unfamiliar with the gruesome and disastrous sequence of events can find out about them in any one of the countless histories written about the affair: how the celebrated Civil War hero, George Armstrong Custer, whose eagerness for battlefield laurels blinded him to every basic law of military engagement and common sense; how he rushed into hostile territory ahead of the main force; how he deployed against an enemy without proper intelligence, splitting his forces in unknown terrain into three against vastly superior numbers; how the doomed men under his command were killed by enraged braves from the Sioux and Cheyenne; and how those wounded could only watch as the bodies of their slain comrades were hacked apart the victorious braves. Their screams and entreaties filled the big Montana sky as the bloody hatchets were finally turned against them. Not a single U.S. soldier survived to tell the story of Custer's Last Stand, but the shock and horror of the soldiers who found upon the mutilated corpses, stripped naked, bloated and bleeding into the thin Montana soil, carried the engagement into the darkest pages of American legend.

Their bodies were promptly buried where they were found, their tombstones clustered atop Last Stand Hill, forming the heart of what would eventually be the Little

Bighorn Battlefield National Monument. Thus, their remains have been interred and their sacrifices honored, but according to many, their spirits remain cursed to a perpetual restlessness, roaming eternally over the ground where they died.

Legend informs us that the Sioux and Cheyenne who rode them down intended such a thing—their vengeance demanded it. They hacked the soldiers' bodies beyond recognition with the belief that the spirits of men whose earthly remains were mutilated would not be able to ascend to heaven. In the years that followed, the Crow Indians from the surrounding reservation spoke of how the country around the Little Bighorn was haunted by the spirits of the dead soldiers. They spoke as though they *knew* it as a fact and seemed to assume the reservation agents knew as well. They called the cemetery supervisor in the Stone House the "ghost herder" because he summoned and released the soldiers' spirits with the daily flag-raising ceremony. When he lowered the flag over the cemetery at sunset, he was setting them free to roam the earth for the night. And every morning, when he hoisted up the Stars and Stripes, he was summoning them back to their graves.

While ghost herding was surely not on the cemetery supervisor's job description, countless testimonials of bizarre experiences through the years suggest that the Crow may have been onto something. Spectral Indian riders have appeared at dusk, and the din of battle—war cries, panic and gunfire—can be heard faint and far on blustery days. More than one park employee has claimed to have come face to face with a pale and grim-faced cavalryman in anachronistic military dress. Startled visitors have claimed the same, both on the wide, open expanse of the battlefield, as well as the in the halls and rooms of the visitor center. Indeed, by all accounts, the battlefield museum is another hotbed of paranormal activity.

Employees going through closing duties have spoke of the transparent likeness of Custer walking through the exhibits. Sometimes he is seen dressed in the buckskin he wore the day of his last battle, on other occasions he is in full military regalia, bedecked in rich blue and shining brass. But always his face is the same, with the bushy handlebar mustache and bright, sorrowful eyes. He is sighted for several seconds, never more, pacing among the tables with a preoccupied and nervous air before fading into nothingness. Though he has never gone out of his way to confront startled onlookers, no one who has seen Custer in the visitor center considers it a pleasant experience. For the feeling he evokes is always the same, filling witnesses with an inexplicable and deep-seated dread, often accompanied by a wave of nausea or a deep chill. Thus, while Custer is never overtly hostile, his psychic manifestation, perhaps a distillation of mortal trauma, shame and defeat, is never a positive thing to encounter. All of the above are purported hauntings that have been experienced on and around Last Stand Hill. Not all the ghosts of the Little Bighorn, however, are bound to the site of the hasty lieutenant colonel's demise.

Major Marcus Reno's Fight

George Armstrong Custer did not initiate the fighting on that fateful June day. Acting on his commanding officer's orders, Major Marcus Reno was the man who launched the first raid of the suicidal attack against the southern end of the enormous Indian encampment. Reno and his men struck around 3 o'clock in the afternoon, their foray into the village intended as the southern point of the pincer movement that Custer had planned. In laying out his strategy, Custer may have imagined Reno and his men riding deep into a poorly defended mass, sending men, women and children reeling in a panicked rout.

Instead, it was Reno's contingent that was sent reeling back before a fierce Sioux counterattack. It came quickly, marking the extent of Reno's anemic assault on the Indian settlement. Less than an hour after they had charged in, Reno's men were engaged in a desperate retreat, galloping out under heavy fire, through deep ravines and finally back across the Little Bighorn. The part of the river they frantically dashed across has come to be called Reno's Crossing, where, carrying or dragging what wounded they could, they braved the withering fire of Indian rifles to scramble up the hills on the opposite bank. There, they dug in and made their stand against the oncoming wave of mounted braves. Unlike Custer and the cavalry under his command, Reno's unit survived the onslaught, though they paid a heavy price.

Along with Last Stand Hill, the cemetery and the visitor center, Reno's Crossing is one of the big attractions for history buffs visiting the battlefield. The same can be said of paranormal enthusiasts hoping to experience something of the weird goings-on long associated with the legendary battlefield. For the many and varied phenomena reported at Little Bighorn, Reno's Crossing is believed to be the place where they occur with the greatest frequency.

In the winter of 2004, a Vietnam veteran who goes by the pseudonym "Jason Davies" took the time to speak about his recent experiences at Reno's Crossing: "I'm not sure how to put it," Davies began. "The trip to the Little Bighorn Battlefield was nothing like I thought it would be. I knew everything about the battle when I went, and I guess I was expecting the ground where they fought to feel, I don't know, *familiar*. But the thing is, the moment my wife and I got out of the car at the National Monument, what I was most aware of was just how strange the place felt. It was everywhere, in the air. This *heaviness*. It was like nothing I'd ever felt before."

The feeling was tangible enough for Davies to mention it to his wife, but she was not feeling the same thing. "I asked her if there was anything about the place that spooked her out. She just looked at me like I was nuts, so I let it go." Or he tried. Intent as Davies was to ignore the foreboding he sensed in the air, it did not loosen its hold on him. If anything, it only got worse with every passing hour.

"Things were weird at the cemetery, for sure. When I say weird, I mean...and this is gonna sound weird...that there were *others* there. And I don't mean other people who made the trip to see the battlefield." By the time the sun touched the horizon, Davies' intangible sense of foreboding took on more substantial manifestations.

"We were in the cemetery for just a few minutes when things started to get really spooky. This is going to sound crazy." Davies hesitated, his voice taking on a somber gravitas that was not there before. "I started hearing voices. They were men's voices; there were actually quite a few of them. All of them were speaking at the same time, and there were too many voices, all speaking way too softly for me to really make out what they were saying. But I'll tell you right now that none of these men were too happy about their situation."

Davis grew more unsettled as the sun set. In his peripheral vision, Davies began to see something moving. "I was just standing there like some kind of zombie, floored by everything going on around me. I mean, first there were these voices, so many of these guys whispering to me. Some of them were scared, others were angry and others were in pain. And then there were the shapes. I swore I saw them—men in dark uniforms, moving slowly toward me out of the corner of my eyes. But whenever I turned to get a good look at them, they would vanish. There was nothing there."

While this was occurring, Davies' wife had been walking ahead of her husband, going through the cemetery on her own pace. She was humming quietly to herself, oblivious to whatever her husband was experiencing. Then she turned around and saw her husband—slack-jawed, ashen, awestruck, with an erratic gaze looking at wonders she could only guess at—it made her blood run cold.

"I can only imagine what I must have looked like," Davies said. "Because my wife looked at me like she had just snapped me out of a coma. She was worried and asked me what was wrong. I was going to tell her about the voices, but I took a look at her and decided that it might not be the best thing to do. So I tried to shrug the whole thing off and just told her something about how the cemetery jogged some memories about 'Nam."

This encounter was not the end of the Davies' experiences at Little Bighorn. "We ended up getting to the battlefield kind of late the first day," Davies said, "so we decided to save the rest of it for the next day. We walked through the museum, went out to take a look at Last Stand Hill and then went out to Reno's Crossing."

At this point, Davies pauses for a moment. When he begins, his tone becomes more hesitant and grave. "Now in spite of everything I've told you, I've gotta say I've never been one to think about ghosts or the afterlife or anything like that. It wasn't that I didn't believe, I just never got around to thinking about those sorts of things. And then the whole thing at Little Bighorn happened, and lately, it's all I've been able to think about, especially after what I saw at Reno's Crossing.

"Things felt better when we got up the next day. They have an outstanding museum there, with more than enough to satisfy the historical enthusiast in me, and there wasn't a cloud in the sky when we walked out to Last Stand Hill." That morning, with the big blue sky and sun shining bright, the weird happenings from the night before seemed like a strange and distant dream. And so they set out to Reno's Crossing. "I guess I just wanted to forget it. I'm not a kid anymore, you know? I'm soft in the middle. I wasn't ready to accept any big new revelations."

Nevertheless, whether he was ready or not, big, new revelations were on their way. "I remember that the sounds started almost the moment we were close enough to the

Little Bighorn to hear its waters flowing. I'll always associate those sounds with that river. And when I think back, the rifle fire, shouts, screams and war whoops are inseparable from the sound of running water."

It was a brilliant Montana morning, but a different world prevailed in the wooded ravines flanking the river. "It suddenly got cooler when we got close to the river, cooler and darker, and then the sounds started. They were faint at first, but they got louder with every step we took toward the river." Freely admitting that he was frightened in the cemetery the night before, Davies claims that he was able to look beyond his fear that morning. "I don't remember feeling nearly as much fear in Reno's Crossing as I did at the cemetery. More than anything else, I think I was curious, even excited."

This sudden thrill came with the realization that, there, on that windblown battlefield, he might be experiencing American history in a way that he would have never thought possible. It occurred to him that if the phenomena he was witnessing were, indeed, supernatural manifestations of the historical 1876 battle, then he wanted to see as much as he could. All at once, Davies resolved to ignore the chill creeping up the back of his neck and picked up his pace, walking to the river, carefully observing his surroundings as he went.

"On some instinctual level, I'm sure I wanted to get out of there. My palms were sweaty, my heart was pounding and the adrenaline was pumping. It was like my body was telling me to turn around and run. And this time, I wasn't the only one that was feeling it." While Davies says that his wife didn't hear the sounds of battle the way he did, it was obvious that she was becoming uneasy as they approached

"It suddenly got cooler when we got closer to the river, cooler and darker, and then the sounds started."

the river. "To this very day, she won't talk about the Little Bighorn River, except to say that she just got a bad case of the 'creeps' when we walked up Reno's Crossing."

Davies has no problems going into greater detail: "My heart stopped when we got to the river's edge. There, on the other side of the Little Bighorn, there was this soldier, an officer, I think. He had red hair and a short red beard. He was just standing there, in the trees, staring at me. I could tell right off that he wasn't real or maybe I should say not *alive*, anyway. He looked sad, like he was saying bye for good, and even though he didn't know who I was, he was still sad about it."

Davies is not sure how long he stood there, transfixed by the man on the other side of the river. "Sometimes when I think back to it, I'll think it might have been five minutes or so, but other times, I swear, he was only there for a few seconds. My wife doesn't know either, because she actually turned around before the riverbank and waited for me a few yards back. Well, however long it was, he vanished—there one second, gone the next. Just like that."

Davies and his wife spent one more day at the battlefield before returning home. Neither has spoken much about what happened during their visit to the Little Bighorn Battlefield. According to Mr. Davies, his wife was plain unwilling to talk about what had happened near Reno's Crossing, and she would much rather forget about it all together. For his part, Mr. Davies learned to keep quiet, not talking to anyone about the experience for years, unsure about how friends and family would react if he began ranting about ghostly battles and the manifestations of soldiers who died in the last century. "My kids already think I'm getting a bit strange in my old age," Davies jokes, "I throw info like this at 'em, they'd write me off all together."

One conversation with Jason Davies and it's clear that he isn't a befuddled old man but someone who's trying to come to grips with the incredible things he has experienced. Why did they appear to him and not to his wife? Did his experiences in Vietnam make him more likely to see the battlefield ghosts? Why have other visitors, people who have never fought on a battlefield, had run-ins with the ghosts there? Indeed, why do some people see the ghosts and others do not? Are the sprits at Little Bighorn trying to say something? Or are they just lost souls still reeling from the trauma of their demise? These are questions that Davies might never find answers to, but his world has been changed because of them. "Everything was different after our trip to Little Bighorn," Davies says. "It's been a few years now, but I still think about what I saw in Montana—all those lost souls still roaming over the battlefield where they were killed. All my life, I've never been very religious, but since our trip in '98, I've taken to praying every now and then. I pray for my wife and my kids and myself and for all those men who were killed out on the Little Bighorn. I hope that one day they find some peace."

3
Old
West

Of Mines and Fires

Jerry and his shift partner stood at the top of the mining shaft, turning their faces to the cool wind blowing across the hills, breathing deeply as the lift rumbled up from the depths.

"Now, you boys, listen here." It was the shift manager. "Before you start, we need you to take a gander at a cave-in reported last night. Word has it that it was just a small one, about 400 feet down."

Jerry and the other miner grunted their response. They had already been told about what had happened, and neither liked to talk too much about cave-ins before starting a day of work. Anyway, there was no use talking about it. It was part of the job. Had to be done. *Make sure the mess got cleaned up,* Jerry thought. *Little side-job. No problem.*

The lift came to the surface with a bang and a clatter, and the two miners got on in silence, followed by the shift manager, who slid the gate shut and took the controls. The lift lurched to life with another bang and a screech, descending with the three men into the darkness of the mine.

"I heard last night was quite the show," the shift manager hollered over the grinding machinery of the lift. "About an hour before the cave-in, the bell rang at 1200 feet."

"Bell rang—so what?" the miner beside Jerry hollered back.

"Thing is, there was nobody working that deep down," the manager said. "They sent the lift down. Brought it back up. Nobody was on board. The shift boss went down there himself to take a look."

"And?" Jerry said.

"Well, all I heard was that the man came back up tight-lipped and strange," the manager replied. "Didn't say much of anything to anyone, but his skin was a shade too white for normal. Cave-in happened a few minutes after that."

Jerry shrugged. He'd been a miner for most of his life, having worked the Maritimes and the Appalachians before moving West. He had been in Butte for no more than a year, but he quickly learned that the miners on the frontier were just as superstitious as they were back East. There were just as many disembodied whispers, giggles and footsteps in the darkness, just as many mysterious shadows and inexplicable lights—and just as many tight-lipped miners carrying their Old World folktales down into the tunnels with them. The lift jolted to a halt.

"Here it is," the shift manager said. "400 feet."

The three men stepped off the lift and immediately saw that something was wrong. There were no lights on. The bulbs lining the tunnel were out, and the path ahead was absolutely dark, swallowing the feeble light of their three headlamps.

"What in the hell?" asked Jerry's mining partner. "Anybody say anything about a short?"

"I didn't hear anything," the shift manager said, also speaking lowly, as though the pitch black was some kind of wild beast he dared not provoke.

Jerry's voice broke the deferential hush. "Well, lights must have went out sometime last night," he said. "Could have had something to do with the accident. Best that we give the place a once-over before getting to work."

The nonchalant statement seemed to break the tension. He knew that, sometimes, down there in the darkness, all a man needed was a reminder of the facts. He had seen it happen many times before. The way the small spaces beneath the surface could close in on a miner, the way the blackness came to life—panic would come on suddenly, but it was nothing more than a figment of the imagination, strained by the hard pressures of mining. It was a part of the job.

"Let's get to it, then," the shift manager spoke up, steadied once more.

The trio stepped from the cage into the black of the unlit tunnel, picking their way carefully through the blackness. They walked in silence, for 30 or 40 feet, when the lights from their helmets revealed a most unexpected site: a mound of rubble and splintered timbers blocked the way, the cave-in from the night before. The men of the previous shift had left it there, untouched. "Well, will you look at this!" the shift manager exclaimed. "Them damn fools must have been right drunk or plain stupid to leave their mess lying here. Someone's going to hear about this, and I mean right now."

Jerry was blinded by light, as the shift manager turned to face him. "Look here, Jerry. I'm going up to report this mess. Youngster here is coming with me; he'll look into getting the electrician to do something about the lights double-quick. You okay with getting to work on this mess by yourself? Shouldn't be gone for more than a few minutes."

Jerry was not thrilled by the prospect of shoveling rock in the dark by himself, but he wasn't about to object. It was part of the job after all. "Sure," he grumbled. "Just don't take your sweet time about it. No way I'm gonna clean this mess all by myself."

The shift manager assured Jerry that they would be back before long, and after handing him a small battery-powered lantern, he turned back toward the lift, leaving the young miner behind him. "Don't worry about the dark, either," the shift manager called back. "The lights oughta come back on before we get back down." Then the two of them continued into the darkness, leaving Jerry there alone. Grumbling under his breath, he switched on the lantern, laid it on the ground, and started moving the rubble.

He heard the lift clamoring up the shaft, and then all was quiet, save for the crunch of his shovel into rock and the steady cadence of his labored breath. He concentrated on the work, doing his best not to dwell on the fact that he was in a tunnel alone 400 feet underground. He was a miner, after all. It was all part of the job.

Evoking the simple tenets of his ever-present work ethic lent him a little comfort, until, that is, the silence in the tunnel was broken by the faint sound of timber popping from somewhere behind the rubble. Not the most comforting to sound to miners, but neither would it have been too uncommon. Jerry looked wearily at the walls, swallowed hard and kept shoveling. "No sweat," he muttered. "The lights'll be back on in no time."

As though on cue, his vision began to flutter. For a brief panic-stricken instant, he thought he was going blind and then he realized that *both* his lights, the one on his helmet and the one on the lantern on the ground, were flickering on and off—at exactly the same time. *Impossible*, he told himself. There was no way both lights could be dying, and it was even less possible for their circuits to be failing simultaneously, but they were, like someone had them both connected to a single switch and was flicking it on and off.

So he was not going blind, but a new panic welled up nevertheless. He straightened up in the strobing tunnel, with a shovel hanging limply at his side, trying to keep his thoughts together amid the completely disorienting flashing. He did not bother wondering what was going on. He only knew that there was no way he would be able to continue to dig rock, not like this. It was time to pick up the blinking lantern, turn around and head back to the lift.

Determined as he was to maintain his composure, to remain calm and collected, Jerry did not run but began to walk slowly and carefully back to the shaft, as the tunnel oscillated between ink black and dimly lit. "Some kind of damn freak light issue here," Jerry said aloud nervously—his voice was strained and sounded almost foreign to his own ears.

And then there was another sound coming from the tunnel behind him. It was the sound of water splashing, as though footsteps were treading through puddles. *Impossible*, Jerry thought, turning to take a better look. He had worked this mine for a while now and knew for a fact that there was no water in these tunnels. He also knew, with even greater certainty, that it was physically impossible for anyone to be behind him—that there could be nothing, *nothing*, between him and the mound of rocks he had been shoveling. He spun around anyway, squinting into the still strobing tunnel, looking for whatever made the noise.

There was nothing but the empty tunnel. "What the devil is going on in this godforsaken place," Jerry muttered, jutting his head back and squinting into the darkness. *What if he has missed something? What if there was a man hurt back there?* "Is there anybody there?" he finally called out.

Jerry held his breath, poised on the balls of his feet, leaning forward toward the direction of the sound, but he heard nothing else. He finally exhaled and decided to continue on to the lift, until, in the next moment, a heavy hand dug its finger into his shoulder. In an instant, everything changed for Jerry, and he couldn't believe his eyes.

There, hovering in the air before him, was a man. Or, it wasn't a man, exactly, but an ashen face atop of a torso without legs or arms. Horrifically lifeless, it hovered until its eyes were level with Jerry's, just inches away, with a sickening grin that revealed a row of long, yellow teeth. Reality, as Jerry understood it, had crumbled. For a second, he was paralyzed by fear, and then, in a flash, Jerry was gone. Squeezing past the hovering torso, he sprinted down the tunnel for the lift. His screams could be heard echoing through the mine.

The thing was right behind him. It made no sound as it flew, but when Jerry looked over his shoulder, he saw that its grin had widened to ghastly proportions—long teeth stretched between thin lips. And while it had no arms or legs, there was no doubt in Jerry's mind that this thing was dangerous—whatever it was and whatever it was doing down there in the mine, he knew its intentions were not good.

He reached the lift at a full run and began frantically ringing for the hoist. The response was quick, as the lift started almost as soon as he hit the bell. But it was not quick enough. Spinning around, Jerry saw that the hovering torso had also made it onto the lift and was now hovering less than a foot away. He reacted, grabbing the bars of the lift and lunging out with his foot, planting his boot solidly in the center of the grinning thing's chest.

It was still grinning, even after the impact of the kick sent it flying off the lift. Raised to safety, Jerry collapsed in a trembling heap, overwhelmed by the adrenaline still coursing through his veins. On the floor, he rolled over to look down the black pit. The sight below almost made Jerry retch. The torso was still there, in the shaft, just several feet away, except now its glassy grin was replaced by a hateful glare. It kept up with the lift for a hundred feet or so, before it gradually vanished into the darkness of the mining shaft.

Jerry was lying on the floor of the lift when it reached the surface. A group of concerned coworkers quickly crowded around him, but he was incapable of answering any of their questions. He just lay there, wide-eyed and slack-jawed—trying, and failing, to come to terms with what he had just gone through.

He was never able to put the incident behind him. He spent the next few weeks in a hospital bed, not saying a word to anyone about the torso in the mine. While he would eventually regain enough composure to go out into the world again, the hardheaded miner would never again venture underground. He spent the rest of his time in Butte working as a watchman for one of the mining companies.

Jerry became known as a very quiet man after his experience, clamming up when people asked him about what went happened. But he must have told at least one person about what he saw, for the story eventually became known throughout town, reported by a Finnish miner named

Waino Nyland in the pages of *Scribner's Magazine* in May 1934.

*   *   *

The tale of Jerry and the flying torso is not the only one to emerge from the mines of Butte, a city that owes its existence (as well as the lion's share of its tragedies) to these subterranean enterprises. The first miners arrived in the 1860s, a scraggily scattering of desperate fortune seekers who set up their modest operations along the hills and gulches of the future townsite. But it turned out that Butte was no Bannack or Virginia City. The ore was difficult to extract and the sources of water needed for the miners' placer operations were scarce.

It would not be until the mid-1870s, when entrepreneurs began cluing in to the profitability of copper and silver, that major mining activity began in earnest. The pursuit for mineral wealth under Butte was massive in scale, creating a network of literally thousands of miles of tunnels under its streets, the furthest extending 5000 feet beneath the townsite. Butte's prominence rose with the surging demand for copper in the late 19th century, and the ramshackle mountain town grew into a major industrial center.

In this sense, Butte is one of the great success stories of Western settlement, but the achievement came at enormous costs. A fortune came out of the mines, but so did environmental degradation, such as the infamous toxic slew called Berkeley Pit, and inhuman labor conditions that had miners facing the dangers of cave-ins, fires, explosions, electrocution and rock dust inhalation. And like

View of the Berkeley Pit

practically every mining town across the United States, Butte would see its share of industrial calamities.

The worst hard rock mining disaster in the United States occurred in Butte. It was June 8, 1917, when an underground lamp in the Granite Mountain shaft of

North Butte Mining Company's Speculator Mine flared up, setting the tunnels' electrical insulation ablaze. The fire spread quickly; noxious gasses flooded the mine. By the time the rescue crews were able to get inside, there were over 160 dead bodies to collect. Some of the men had died almost immediately on the sites they worked. Others lived longer, managing to complete good-bye letters to their loved ones as they slowly suffocated.

The Granite Mountain shaft was shut down after the incident, and a monument was later erected on the hilltop that looked out over the shaft. When the mine reopened 23 years later, the first miners to go down were not too happy about it. The stories began to circulate about the spirits' unrest—the mournful whispers in the dark, the shadows moving sluggishly against the greater darkness and the tortured wheezing of unseen men gasping for breath.

The Royal Milling Fire and the Quartz Street Station

The call went out on January 15, 1895. There was a fire in a warehouse in South Butte belonging to the Royal Milling Company. A group of professional firemen and volunteers was hastily organized and sent out. There was nothing unusual about this fire; Butte was already a burgeoning industrial town, and there had been fires before, but no one could have foreseen the events that followed.

The firefighting crew descended on the scene, not knowing that large, unregistered stores of blasting powder were boxed up in the nearby Butte Hardware Company and Kenyon-Connell Commercial Company warehouses. Fire Chief Angus Cameron had an entire unit deployed when the first flames reached the blasting powder. The ensuing explosion was felt all across Butte. For miles around, people could see the metal roof of the Kenyon-Connell building go spinning some 100 feet into the sky. Over 35 people were instantly killed in the initial blast, ripped to pieces by the roaring force of the fire.

Witnesses immediately came running to help, but those who arrived too soon fell victim to two more explosions that followed minutes after the first. Pipes and iron bars stored in the warehouse became deadly shards of shrapnel. Metal barrels were torn open and sent flying with their highly flammable contents burning out of control. The screams of maimed and dying casualties echoed through the streets of Butte.

No one who was there could have ever forgotten the smoldering gore after the smoke had settled. It was estimated that 57 people perished in the explosion. No one could say for certain because many corpses were nothing more than charred and unidentifiable body parts, and there was still no reliable census of the citizens in Butte. Fifty-seven, they said, more or less, including the mutilated bodies of the fire chief, the assistant chief and the 11 firemen who served under them. Three of Butte's firefighting corps survived the explosion, and only because they had the good fortune of being delayed on their way to the site.

One of the three surviving firemen was a German-American named Pete Sanger. Blessed as everyone told him he was, Sanger had difficulties accepting his good fortune. Haunted by the fate of his coworkers, unable to find meaning in his survival, Sanger threw himself into his work, turning it into his mission, which revolutionized the administration and execution of firefighting in Montana's booming mining center. (The municipal authorities helped his cause by making a revamped fire department one of their highest priorities.) Another disaster like Royal Milling was to be avoided at all costs, and if it meant investing money to modernize firefighting facilities, then so be it.

Sanger had arrived in Butte in 1888. A townsman with a wife and an eye for opportunity, he opened up a barbershop and took up a volunteer position with Butte's firefighters. In the wake of the 1895 explosion, he joined on as a full-time member in the suddenly depleted force, and in four years time, he was appointed chief of the department. His tenure brought much change. The first thing he did was hire more firemen, swelling the force's ranks to unprecedented numbers. With his experience as a veteran firefighting volunteer in towns across the West, Sanger understood the necessity of rapid response, and to this purpose, set up two more fire stations on Arizona Street and Caledonia Street, respectively, while the Quartz Street Station, built in 1900, was designated as the department's headquarters.

The building on Quartz was the first of its kind in Butte. A fully equipped fire station, it lodged 22 men, not including Sanger and his family. Close to the station, Sanger commissioned the construction of a tower, where his men ran drills and trained in a modern gymnasium. Sanger worked to consolidate the professional status of firefighters in Butte and became a vocal member of national and state firefighting associations, tirelessly lobbying in favor of a pension for his men. In every way he could, Sanger fought to legitimize his vocation and ended up changing what it was to be a fireman in Butte, so by 1905, there were 41 firefighters across town.

While Sanger prospered publicly, securing practically every improvement he went after, his personal life was marked by tragedy and grief. In 1904, after a lengthy struggle with cancer, his wife Margaret succumbed to her illness, breathing her last in her bedroom on the top floor of the Quartz Street Station. Mrs. Sanger had long been like a den mother to the firefighters, as they went about their dangerous work. When her body was taken from her deathbed, it was lovingly borne at the head of a long procession of firefighters and citizens; her last passage through the streets of Butte trailed by mourners and carriages laden with flowers.

Not two years later, Sanger was dealing with another loss, when his daughter, Hazel, fell ill at the Dillon boarding school she attended. She was suddenly bedridden, and Sanger and his son rushed to Dillon as soon as they were able, but as it turned out, they arrived 40 minutes too late. Hazel Sanger was dead of peritonitis at 18 years of age.

It was the last heartache Sanger would endure. Two years later, he married again; her name was Louisa, and she was a gentle woman who cared deeply for her husband. When another burning building called him to duty, she would perch herself on a chair before the upstairs window to watch over her husband and his crew until they safely returned. Passersby came to take her presence at the window as a sure announcement that a fire was raging somewhere in Butte.

Her husband always returned to receive her greeting. Sometimes he was a little banged up, having suffered from some minor burn or smoke inhalation, but it was never anything he couldn't walk off. But on January 11, 1915, when the alarm sounded a fire on the other side of town, Sanger and three of his men jumped into a wagon and sped out onto the streets of Butte. Unfortunately, they never made it to the fire.

Sources say they were going at about 40 miles an hour when the fire truck ran straight into a Walkerville streetcar. The collision sent all four men in the wagon flying, but in the aftermath of the wreckage, Sanger was the only one who was not able to get back to his feet. The three firemen acted quickly, picking up the bleeding and barely conscious chief and carrying him back to the Quartz Street Station. Louisa had already heard about the collision. She was waiting on the ground floor for the men to return—it was the first time she had abandoned her post at the window before the wagon returned. Regaining consciousness, Sanger had become livelier but was still bleeding heavily from the head, and for the most part, he spoke in mumbled gibberish. The doctor at the scene promptly diagnosed a head trauma, a concussion and hemorrhage, but he was not able to treat these injuries.

Incredibly, Butte's fire chief held on for weeks, long enough for Louisa to secure the services of a surgeon in San José. Louisa remained stubbornly hopeful, but Sanger himself was more pessimistic about his recovery and made a point to bid farewell to his wife and accompanying friends, as the train rumbled toward San José. Just before surgery, Sanger reportedly told his friend, San José Fire Chief Edward Haley: "Do what you can for my wife. I am in bad shape…and I feel that I will have to go over the hurdles." The two parted with a handshake, and Sanger died of complications on the operating table.

Louisa made the trip back to Butte with her husband's body, stoically overseeing his burial, where he was interred next to his first wife and his daughter. There was little comfort for her there after that, and she did not stay on in Butte for long, moving to Los Angeles as soon as she was able. Little is known of her life after that, though if some of the tales about the Quartz Street Station are true, there may be reason to believe that, in the end, some part of her decided to make Butte her final resting place.

As grief-stricken as the community was at the death of its passionate fire chief, the work of Butte's firemen did not stop with Peter Sanger's passing. Life went on, and work continued at Quartz Street, as it would throughout much of the 20th century. Finally deemed obsolete in the

1980s, the station became the home of the Butte-Silver Bow Public Archives.

Regional history buffs will be grateful that the Quartz Street Station's past was not lost with the transformation. The historic structure still bears the mark of Peter Sanger's constant drive for innovation, with the then-new fangled electric alarm boxes installed by the former chief still mounted on walls throughout the building. On the ground floor, the firemen's kitchen remains much as it was when Chief Sanger ran the local show. The original stables have also remained remarkably well preserved. The stalls where the fire crews maintained their vehicles—from fire horses early on to the ever more powerful engines that replaced them—are still there, in the darkened recesses of the building's lower floor.

It is likely that this lower, infrequently visited section of the building would be forgotten all together, if not for the strange occurrences frequently reported from within. Over the years, a number of employees at the archives have reportedly been distracted from their work by inexplicable noises in the empty stables below—the jovial sound of men talking and laughing. It is muffled, as though it is heard from some distance, and yet it is always coming from the old stables, which is impossible because there is never anyone there.

It probably comes as no surprise that the general conclusion involves the possibility of ghosts or spirits of a number of Butte's early firemen haunting the building. For the many who have claimed to hear the voices of these long-dead men, they all insist that there is nothing foreboding about the experience. By the sound of the voices, there is a sense that the men in the stables are there because they want to be. No one has ever been able to make out exactly what they are saying, but it is apparently obvious to all that they are having a good time, mixing it up in some grand, boisterous and highly exclusive re-union. There is no record of anyone ever feeling even vaguely threatened or uneasy by this occasional ghostly fête.

If anything, the spirits that haunt the old Quartz Street Station are said to leave a calming, even pleasant, impression on those who have sensed them. According to legend, this is especially the case upstairs, where the fire chief's apartment rooms were once located. Ellen Baumler is the author of *Spirit Tailings: Ghost Tales from Virginia City, Butte, and Helena*, one of the seminal works of the paranormal in Montana. She describes the sense of "welcome that is difficult to define."

Others might not hesitate in trying to describe it: the warm feeling of goodwill can be nothing other than the residual energy of the Sanger family, happy to be united in death after all the tragedies they had endured in life. While this may very well be the case, one cannot help but wonder *which* Sanger family is enjoying such a blissful time at the Quartz Street Station. For we must not forget that Sanger had been married twice, and both his wives, if there is any truth to the accounts, were equally devoted to the station's first fire chief. Are the spirits of both Mrs. Sangers content to reside with one another, or has only one of the fire chief's wives remained behind? While there is no small measure of absurdity in such speculation, the prevailing theory has the presence of Louisa Sanger as the surest bet—surest because, in all the accounts of goings-on at the

Quartz Street Station, the only sighting of a visual apparition was most likely that of Mr. Sanger's second wife.

Ms. Balmer reports the account in her aforementioned work. While leaving the old station after work, the Butte-Silver Bow Archives director happened to look back at the building while she was unlocking her car. There, on the top-floor window overlooking the parking lot, was an elderly woman standing with a dish towel in her hands. She was there and gone in a span of seconds. The director had blinked once, and the woman was no longer there. Assuming that she had imagined the vision, she got in her car and went home, thinking nothing more of the experience until she stumbled on an old photograph of Louisa Sanger. And she recognized her immediately as the woman standing at the top floor. She had even been standing at the exact same window.

Like so many other purportedly haunted sites, the reported phenomena at the old fire station did little to clarify what is happening there, and why. Could Peter Sanger, who loved his work so much while he was alive, still be present in one form or another, in the Quartz Street Station? Is he upstairs, contributing to the sense of calm and well being reported there? Or maybe he is leading the carousing reported in the basement and Louisa is the spirit haunting the second floor. But then, the spirit could also be Margaret, who actually died on the second floor. It is impossible to say, but whatever is going on, it seems to be a positive thing, which is remarkable, given all the death and tragedy the Sangers had faced during their time in Butte. Indeed, the supposed supernatural situation at the Quartz Street Building could be far worse.

Jack and Virginia Slade and the Phantoms of Virginia City

Strung up on the corral fence, Jules Benni was writhing under a hellfire sun of a Wyoming August. His left eye was blackened and swollen, his tongue was drooping from sagging lips and a mass of congealed blood spread over the dirty fabric of his shirt. The garment was punctured at the side, where several pellets from a shotgun had found their mark. It was just a few days previous in Pacific Springs, when a bounty hunter got the jump on big, mean Jules Benni, clipping him with one barrel of buckshot, as he stumbled half-drunk out of a frontier saloon. Jules fell where he stood—wounded but not killed. Without a word of explanation, he was strapped to the back of a horse and taken to meet the man who had put the price on his head. He was brought to the home of the infamous six-gun menace, Jack Slade. What followed was the darkest, meanest, most brutal chapter of the legendary gunfighter's story.

Unfortunately for Jules Benni, Jack was drunk when the big man was dragged to his doorstep, and everyone knew what Jack Slade was like when he was floundering in his cups: mischievous, if he was in a good mood; homicidal, if he was not. The problem was that Benni had shot Jack full of holes just two years earlier. And while Jack Slade had miraculously survived the attack, he could not forget what Jules had done to him. Jules Benni's arrival, then, did not put him in the best of moods.

Or maybe it would be more accurate to say that it put him in the best possible mood. That's the way it would have looked to the bounty hunter who delivered the wounded man. Slade immediately lit up at the sight of his unconscious nemesis. "Well, look here!" Slade exclaimed with a smile that might have made Jules very concerned for his immediate future, had he been awake. "If it ain't the dog himself! Never thought you'd see this face again, did you, Jules?"

Receiving not so much as a grunt in reply, Slade's face dropped. He looked to the bounty hunter. "Ain't dead, is he?"

"Not last time I checked," said the bounty hunter. "Just lost a bit of blood. God knows we didn't have the easiest trip up."

"That's fine," said Slade. "A little misery builds character."

"That's the truth." The bounty hunter was feeling more than a little uneasy at the ugly leer that had once again broken across Slade's face. He took his pay and left Jules to what he was sure would be a gruesome fate. How gruesome, he dared not guess.

When Jules came to, he was tied to the rough-hewn fence of Slade's corral amid the stench and squeal of a crowded pigpen. Through the haze of semiconsciousness he was aware of the burning pain in his side, the heat from the cloudless sky and his agonizing, searing thirst. He raised his head, opened his eyes and croaked for something, maybe water, maybe help.

What Jules saw in front of him brought the Sunday sermons of his childhood to mind, sermons of final judgment and the ultimate fate of the wicked. There, about 20 yards away, was his mortal enemy, Jack Slade, with a bottle of whiskey in his hands and a psychotic grin beaming across his face. There was a six-shooter strapped to his side and a Winchester rifle propped against a bucket. Jules wondered if he had died and gone to hell. "Slade?" he rasped. "Is that you?"

"Well, I'll be!" shouted Jack Slade. "Look who's come back to us. How you doing, Jules? Comfortable, I hope!"

Jules tried to raise his voice. "Look, Slade, what happened before, that was just a misunderstanding, I can't see no reason why we can't talk it out."

Slade downed the rest of his whiskey in one last gulp before throwing the empty bottle at Jules. The wounded man barely had the strength to jerk his head out of the way as it hit the rail behind him.

"Sure, Jules," Slade said as he reached for his rifle and put it to his shoulder. "Let's talk it out."

After the crack of the rifle report, the panicked squeals of the pigs drowned out Jules' tortured wail. The bullet passed straight though his leg, and the pain was excruiciating. Revived unwillingly, Jules stared across the corral at the man who had just shot him. "My God, Slade! What in damnation are you doing? If killing me is what you're after, then go ahead and be done with it!"

"I don't know about that, partner," Jack Slade said as he pumped the lever of his Winchester. "After all, you didn't let me off that easy the last time we saw each other, now did you?"

"Damn you!" Jules yelled as Slade raised the rifle toward him again. The next bullet tore through Jules shoulder. The one after that pierced his already bloodied side, where the buckshot was embedded. And so Slade kept it up. As a seasoned frontier gunfighter, Slade's aim was sharper the drunker he got. He emptied his Winchester into Jules, careful that no single bullet would be lethal. After that, he drew his six-shooter and opened fire, going for more whiskey at some point, laughing at his own morbid quips, while Jules' tortured screeches became barely audible groans. Massive blood loss and shock had almost robbed Jules Benni of his consciousness when Slade decided he had had enough fun. Pulling his bowie knife from his belt, he strode up to his victim and cut both his ears off, dangling the bloody trophies before Jules' face before putting his revolver to his head and pulling the trigger to end the inhuman torment.

Legend tells us that the heinous torture and murder of Jules Benni occurred in August of 1861, roughly two years after Benni's attempt on Slade's life, and 11 years before Mark Twain immortalized the perpetrator of the crime in *Roughing It.* "An outlaw among outlaws," wrote Twain, "and yet their relentless scourge, Slade was at once the most bloody, the most dangerous and the most valuable citizen that inhabited the savage fastnesses of the mountains."

It seems that this attitude was shared by practically everyone who ever met him. Jack Slade, on one hand, was the undeniably charming frontiersman and on the other, a maniacal man-killer. He was the Jekyll and Hyde of the American West.

At his best, Slade had the highest esteem of his peers, giving free rein to drinking and boisterous behavior when he was among the rough men of the smoky frontier saloons, while being remarkably genteel whenever he was in the company of respectable women. When he was at his

Without fail, Jack Slade was dangerous and violent after his many whiskey-drinking sessions at the local saloon.

best, he was the type of man that others gravitated toward, a natural leader and protector in the dangerous world west of the 100th meridian.

But when his demons emerged, Jack Slade became dangerous, unpredictable, unruly, intemperate and often lethal. He swaggered with lunacy in his eyes and loose guns in his belt, and he was as bad as any murdering gunslinger in the West.

The problem was booze. Slade the sensible frontiersman habitually met Slade the brutish killer in the bottom of a bottle. Without fail, it was the brutal killer who emerged from these whiskey-drinking sessions, roaring at the world, bullying and vandalizing, brandishing shooting irons as though they were toys and sometimes—on the occasions when he was especially far gone—murdering a man or two.

Unless homicidal rages were preferred, it was best that Jack Slade steer clear of alcohol. Certainly his equally famous wife, Virginia Slade, lived a life that should have been a model to Jack. To be clear, Virginia Slade was hardly the picture of propriety, especially for a Victorian woman. Big, bold and always ready to speak her mind, black-haired Virginia was definitely a product of the rough frontier. It was said she always carried a six-shooter strapped beneath her dress and was easily as skilled in its use as her husband was.

Yet free-willed as she was, Virginia Slade was not at all cursed with her husband's unstable disposition. Kind, steady and strong, Virginia was a devoted to Jack, for all his wild tendencies, and, according to some, certainly had a soothing influence on his wilder side. It was said that he always did his best to steer clear from the booze when she was around.

Still, her influence was not soothing enough to keep her husband from getting fired from job with the Overland Stage Company in 1861. Two years later, Jack and Virginia moved north to the rough streets of Virginia City. It was 1863, 26 years before Montana became a state, and Virginia City was one of a handful of settlements that sprung up over night with the discovery of gold. The Slades' new home was as bad as any boomtown in the West, with all the requisite saloons, desperate men and gunfights. It was also the place where Jack Slade would finally meet his end.

Mark Twain wrote that Slade had reportedly killed 26 men in his lifetime, yet considering this brutal (and most probably exaggerated) record, he was remarkably well behaved during his time in Virginia City. At the very least, it is doubtful that anyone died by his hand, but legend does tell us that he still took great joy in the lawlessness of the boomtown and regularly shot the place up during whiskey-soaked benders.

Far from being the ideal law-abiding citizen, Slade did not leave a trail of bodies. Damaged property, however, was another story. With neither second thought nor guilt, Jack routinely put bullets in business signs, windows, barrels, troughs, bar tops and saloon ceilings. When he was raging, Jack would have shouting matches with anyone who struck him as funny. There were no shortage of townsfolk who came out of these confrontations with deep and abiding dislike for the man. While Slade had angered and insulted a number of Virginia City's citizenry, there was a notion in the air that Jack Slade was changing. He was still mean, and when he drank, he associated with the least desirable elements in town. But no one had died by his hand, which was a most definite departure from his past behavior.

It has been said that Virginia Slade may have been responsible for this relative tempering of Jack's disposition. Who knows? If she had had more time, she may have been able to reform him altogether. But then, events were working against the Slades.

The force of public sentiment was changing, when the more orderly residents of Virginia City, Bannack and Nevada City finally decided that they had enough of the violence racking their lawless region. So in the winter of 1863, a lawyer by the name of Wilbur F. Sanders formed a vigilance committee. For several months, the committee acted as the sole law enforcement body in the area. Sanders and his men hunted down criminals, arrested them, tried them and executed them. It was not the best way to dispense justice. They were successful in apprehending and executing a number of known murderers, but then there were others who were accused of crimes that were tenuous at best. During this time, more than one man was hanged simply because the public needed a scapegoat. Others endured punishments completely incommensurate with their crimes. The last man who was sent to this vigilance committee's makeshift gallows was Jack Slade. And in this controversial case, the punishment most definitely did not fit the crime.

In the spring of 1864, Jack Slade, reputed murderer of 26 men, was tried and hanged for upsetting a milk reservoir. There was still snow on the ground that March evening when Jack stumbled out of a bar with a group of sodden acolytes in tow. Thick with drink and bent on mischief, the gang of ne'er-do-wells were set on mischief—in short, a night like any other.

Wanton destruction was imminent, and Slade set his eyes on an unusual target. Apparently, there was something upsetting about the town's milk wagon that night. One look at it sent the drunken Slade into a rage, and to the whoops and cheers of his entourage, he emptied his revolver into it before pushing it over a hill. Not the classiest stunt a man might pull, and Slade could be blamed for far worse. The problem, however, was that the public had been pushed beyond tolerance with the town's lawless elements, and on this particular night, the merciless vigilance committee was riding through the area, looking for excuses to exercise its extreme and unfailing judgment.

Slade was likely still nursing his hangover when news of the destroyed milk wagon spread through town. In his home several miles from town, he was unaware of the general outrage at his senseless act. He destroyed the sole supply of milk for Virginia City and nearby Nevada, and people of both towns would now be deprived for days. When it became known that the man responsible was none other than Jack Slade, the popular response was spontaneous and absolute. Slade had finally used up the town's last ounce of goodwill. He may have been fine when he was sober, but he was not nearly good enough to make up for his stupidity when inebriated. The vigilance committee was called in to do something, and needless to say, something was done.

It was done promptly. The committee apprehended an unwitting Slade the next time he rode into town. He was tried on the same day and found guilty of disturbing the peace. There could be no arguing the verdict, but the sentence went down as one of the great injustices imposed by the committee. The sentence was death, and they did not hesitate to carry it out. In fact, no sooner had the sentence been passed, Slade was dragged down Cover Street to the Elephant Corral, led by a noose and followed by a buzzing crowd.

Slade had a friend or two in the crowd who raced off to the Slade's homestead to tell Virginia what had befallen her husband. When Virginia heard the news, she did not waste a second of her time. Grabbing her pistol and putting heels to her horse, she rode at a galloping pace the entire way to Virginia City, clearing the way with shots of her revolver, desperate to save her beloved Jack.

Unfotunately for Jack Slade, the punishment definitely did not fit the crime.

It was said that Virginia's shouts and gunfire were heard at the edge of town when Jack's executor kicked the crate out from under him. His body was still swinging when the cry went out. "Mrs. Slade's coming!" Everyone there turned to look, and sure enough, there she was—Virginia Slade at the top of the hill, with tears streaming across her face, coming down the road with a smoking gun in one hand and reins in the other. When she saw her dear Jack hanging lifeless, her shriek of grief and rage carried over every street and alley in town.

Some say it is a wonder she did not put her revolver to any further use that day, standing, as she was, before the men who took her husband's life. Perhaps there was some part of her who understood that this was the way Jack would meet his end. Perhaps there was a just inevitability to it, given all the misery he had visited upon others during his lifetime. Surely, Virginia would have been familiar with the biblical proverb about living and dying by the sword. Virginia knew full well what kind of man her husband was, and though she did her best to change his ways, his unfortunate end could not have been a complete surprise.

She was, however, livid that Slade was sentenced to death for destroying a milk wagon. She did not say a word to anyone during the funeral, which turned out to be more of a spectacle than any kind of service. This was, after all, the one and only Jack Slade, the infamous gunfighter who carried the ears of Jules Benni in his pocket. Slade had been a legend on the frontier, and most of the townspeople in attendance were there for the last chapter of the story.

Virginia refused to have her husband buried in the town, so after the service, she placed Jack in a zinc coffin, filled it with whiskey and had it sealed. She would wait until the snow melted before taking Jack's remains to Salt Lake City for what she deemed would be a proper burial. And contrary to popular assumption, this was *not*, in fact, the last chapter of Jack Slade's story.

First, there was Virginia Slade's vengeance to contend with. She singled out one or two townsfolk for being responsible for Jack's death and tormented them, whenever she had the opportunity. Though none suffered any injury at Virginia's hands, there were definitely some tense encounters over the course of the following year, until the former Mrs. Slade met her next husband and moved down to Salt Lake City.

Even then, Virginia City was not rid of the Slades. The first stories to circulate were about the old Slade household. The couple made their home in a ranch in Meadow Valley along the Bozeman Road north of town, where they supplemented their income by charging a toll for passage on that section of the trail. The house went unoccupied after the Slades were gone, abandoned and sagging slowly into decrepitude, becoming home to the local fauna—bats in the rafters, snakes under the floors, voles and raccoons in the rotting corners. Years came and went, but no one forgot that this crumbling building on the Bozeman Road had once been home to the Slades. And no one thought, even for a moment, to clean the place up and move in.

It wasn't just a matter of big renovations, either. The ruins of the Meadow Valley ranch house had acquired a haunted reputation. The tales were first heard from travelers coming into Virginia City late at night. Stumbling into taverns well after dark, these individuals stuttered out bewildering accounts of a glowing figure moving in the old Slade House. Sometimes, they described seeing a figure through the shattered windows, a silvery semitransparent apparition surrounded by a glowing mist. There was no color to be seen, just differing shades of that moonlit gray, but often they spoke of a diminutive frame, sharp facial features and a dead stare. They always described the former Jack Slade.

Others had more immediate experiences, where a shouted challenge came from the inside of the house—a man's voice demanding to know who was passing their house without paying the toll for the road. Those credulous travelers, who believed that there might be someone manning the tollhouse, would stop before the building, wondering who might possibly be living in such a dilapidated house. Always the travelers were left with a frisson of terror, as the shape drifted through the doorway: a short man with dead eyes, shrouded in a glowing mist that obscured the rest of his body. That was as far as the encounter would go, for no man looking upon the apparition at the doorway would linger a second longer. In the last decades of the 19th century, a number of arrivals into Virginia City were breathless men babbling about the figure they had seen emerging from the Meadow Valley house.

There was a skeptical backlash to reports of the ghost of Jack Slade. Doubters brought up the recent rumors that a gang of bandits had been using the abandoned house as a hideout. Was it not convenient, skeptics asked, that this spate of bizarre sightings coincided with word of robbers setting up there? Rational minds were quick to conclude that the supposed ghost of Jack Slade was most likely a legend in the making, perhaps fashioned by the brigands themselves, concocted to keep potential interlopers away. For many townsfolk, this sufficed as a reasonable explanation for the stories about the Slade's former house. Ever after, a perpetual shadow of doubt hung over whatever testimonials emerged.

There was another popular account, however, that stuck much better than the ghost of Meadow Valley. Something would happen on certain nights in the hills just northeast of town, when there was a full moon hung low in the sky. On these nights, a stillness would descend on the land when no nocturnal creature stirred, and there was not even a whisper of a breeze in the air. Those who lived on the outskirts of Virginia City knew that this was the time when Virginia Slade would rise again to relive her tortured ride into town.

The heavy silence was suddenly broken by the distant clatter and thump of a horse approaching at full gallop into town, moving quickly, with the sound of its hooves on the trail growing louder by the second. Something about its staccato beat spreads a chill through anyone who is there to hear them. Then the dust of the approaching rider appears on the road, as though lit from within. Another moment later, the rider and beast come into sight. Virginia Slade, with her big funeral dress billowing around her, is mounted atop a heaving black stallion that is moving too fast for any earthly creature, as it cuts through the countryside.

The creature crests a hill, takes a curve and then comes into sight of Virginia City nestled on the mountain. That is when the sound begins, a deep moan, gathering low and heavy, as though from the earth itself, swelling louder and louder, rising to a high pitch, louder still, until it is a deafening shriek, echoing over the mountains and, once again, down every street and alley in Virginia City, only to be cut off in an instant, all at once. Virginia and her mount, too, have vanished in a blink, leaving nothing but the mountains and the moon and the unnaturally still night.

Boots on the Boardwalk and Other Nevada City Stories

It is said that Charles Bovey, former Montana representative and heir to the General Mills fortune, did not wear cowboy boots. He did, however, have an abiding love for frontier America, so much so that he spent considerable time and money preserving the monuments of the era. Historic Nevada City, located just one mile west of Virginia City, is largely a product of Bovey's passion for the past.

Charlie Bovey and his wife, Sue, were taken with Virginia City on their first visit to the little community in 1944. Soon after, they became dedicated to preserving its historical heritage. With ambitions to initiate a preservation program to rescue the fragile monuments from the town's past, the Boveys began buying what buildings they could. Working in conjunction with the Bovey-financed Montana Historic Landmark Society, they eventually came to own roughly one-third of the buildings in Virginia City.

As for the much smaller ghost town of Nevada City, perhaps Bovey would not have even noticed that it was there if not for the activities of one Montana rancher. The story goes that Bovey was visiting Virginia City sometime in the 1940s, looking for prospective purchases among the crumbling old cabins, when he noticed smoke rising from the west. Heading out to take a look, he learned that a rancher by the name of Lester Stiles was burning a historic cabin because of the danger it posed to his horses. Unable to accept that the handful of other abandoned

19th-century buildings on Stiles' land were destined for the same fiery fate, Bovey negotiated a price for the buildings. And so began the Nevada City project.

The restoration spanned a period of some 30 years. Whenever Bovey would discover a neglected Montana frontier building destined for ruin, he would do what he could to purchase it and move it to Nevada City. The buildings of the expanded ghost town were arranged to form a few streets and then filled with historic artifacts from the Boveys' extensive collections. By the time the Boveys were done, about 80 buildings had been relocated to Nevada City, forming an impressive historical exhibit of frontier structures from varied times and locations across Montana.

Thus, the former ghost town was expanded and elaborated and turned into something of a serious-minded Old West theme park, set in an authentic locale and stocked with real-life structures from the time. Given the popular notion of how spirits that haunt the earthly plane are often bound to the structures they knew, is it any wonder that there are reports of ghostly encounters coming from Nevada City?

For not only does such a concentration of historic buildings beg for hauntings, but so too does the site they are situated on. During its heyday, Nevada City was not the most pleasant place in the world to live. After the discovery of gold in Alder Gulch in 1863, the surrounding area in southern Montana was soon teeming with over 10,000 desperate fortune hunters—young men, largely without prospects, willing to do almost anything for gold. Nevada City and its dissolute sister settlement, Virginia City, practically went up over night, and they were

abandoned just as quickly. The towns' collapse was imminent, once gold was discovered in Helena's Last Chance
Gulch in 1864. Soon after, the promise of richer prospects
began to lure Virginia City and Nevada City miners to
Helena. By the early 1870s, the population along Alder
Gulch was estimated to be nothing more than a few hundred souls. Nevada City was essentially abandoned all
together, while Virginia City clung to existence. Yet
although the region's heyday spanned only a few years,
they were a turbulent few years, replete with all the violence and chaos associated with the American frontier.

Charlie Bovey loved Nevada City. His passions for history and collecting came together in the makeshift ghost
town. It was where he chose to spend most of his spare
time, taking his time strolling the quiet streets between the
abandoned buildings, regularly sleeping in the humble
cabins behind the Nevada City Hotel, despite having his
luxurious home in nearby Virginia City. His favorite place
to be and the place where he died, succumbing to a heart
attack on June 9, 1978, was in Cabin 5.

The historic properties remained in possession of the
Bovey family until 1997, when the State of Montana
bought up the family's holdings in the two former mining
towns. Nevada City remains today, and its five permanent
residents is by no means a reflection of its cultural value to
the state. Seeing anywhere up to 70,000 visitors a year,
Bovey's historical repository is much more than an expression of one man's love for the past. It is also a place where
the past comes to life for thousands of guests every year—
in more ways than one.

While certain testimony asserts that the ghosts of
Nevada City's past do indeed walk its streets, it also seems

as if these ghosts, by and large, tend to avoid the ghost town's peak season. Closed to tourism in the winter months, Nevada City becomes a true ghost town, shrouded in snow and cold, abandoned but for a few state employees who watch over and maintain the historic buildings. One of the early accounts of the strange goings-on came from a park employee who was staying in one of the designated living areas: Cabin 5.

The event took place on a spring evening in 1999; a long winter's chill was still hanging in the air, and the ghost town would not be open for several weeks yet. The state employee sleeping in Cabin 5 was still in winter mode; he had long gotten used to the quiet of his station. In those months, there is not much traffic passing through Nevada City, pedestrian or otherwise. So he was quite astonished to wake up in the middle of the night to the sound of footsteps on the boardwalk outside. The distinct footfalls were plodding, moving across the boardwalk on heavy heels—it was the sound of cowboy boots worn by someone heavy.

The employee hastily threw on some clothes, slipped into his boots and ran out into the cold night, looking for the person who had decided to take a walk through the deserted town at that hour. Outside he did not see anyone, but he could still hear the heavy gait on the boardwalk near the center of town. The employee went after the sound until he got to the entrance of the visitor's center. There, the footsteps suddenly stopped. He braved the cold a little longer, taking a quick tour through the town, but there was no trace of the late-night visitor.

Another employee, who also lived in Cabin 5, claimed to have heard the same footsteps many years before, in the

Cabins in Nevada City

1970s. On this occasion, it was deep in the middle of winter, with snow piled deep along the buildings and around the boardwalk. This employee had also been asleep; he was woken late at night by his dog, growling and standing hunched by the door. Groggy, he was about to check on his dog's behavior when the footsteps began to approach. This employee did not act as quickly as his later counterpart; he remained in bed, quiet as the thud of the heels on the boardwalk slowly approached his cabin and then continued on by. Only several minutes later, when the footsteps could no longer be heard and his dog had calmed down, did the Nevada City employee get out of bed, get dressed and creep out into the night. Not only was there no one there, but there was also no trace of any passage in the snow that surrounded the boardwalk. If there had been a man on the wooden walkway, he would have had to materialize on one end, walk to the other end, and then simply cease to be.

Disembodied footsteps were not the only inexplicable occurrence reported from Nevada City. Much like Nevada City itself, the Nevada City Hotel exists as something of an antique amalgam. The front of the hotel is an old stagecoach stop from the small town of Gaffney, south of Twin Bridges, dating back to the 1860s. Bovey had the stage depot taken apart, transported and then reassembled on the site of the Nevada City Hotel. Another building forms the back of the establishment: a dormitory from the early 20th century that served as a residence for seasonal workers at Yellowstone Park. The stage stop and the dormitory were attached to form the Nevada City Hotel. Whether the ghosts said to reside within are from Gaffney, Yellowstone or just down the street is anyone's guess.

One presence in the hotel that has been noted by a number of guests is the woman in Room 12. The phenomenon plays out the same almost every time. A guest, usually in adjacent Room 11, is distracted from sleep by a sound coming from the other side of the wall. It is a woman, and she is obviously unhappy, crying loudly and continuously through the night. Sometimes the guest in Room 11 manages to fall asleep and sometimes not, but either way, the woman's wailing in the next room have never been interrupted. Be it respect for privacy or simple unwillingness to get involved with a stranger's troubles, no consolation has ever been offered to the woman on the other side of the wall.

Thus, no one can say for certain why she is mourning, though many guests do make a point of telling the receptionist about her the next morning. Expressing concern or irritation, they soon learn that there was no one staying in Room 12. The startled guests are then also told not to worry for their sanity, for they are not the only ones to hear wails coming from the unoccupied room. She has been a resident of the Nevada City Hotel for quite some time.

Another incident involves a film crew that used the old bar in the hotel for a set in the winter of 2001. A few days before the film crew's arrival, a hotel employee named Marge Antolik was taking inventory in the bar when she had some minor difficulties with her tools. A flashlight she had laid down on the bar vanished a moment later, only to be found a few seconds later exactly where she had left it. It was a minor incident, but it left the employee with a certainty that things in the saloon were not quite right. Something was there, a presence that Marge did not understand. As it turned out, this presence loved an audience.

A few days later, the film crew was in place. Fifty or so people were crowded into the Nevada City Hotel's bar: actors, cameramen, gaffers, director and support staff. Marge Antolik was there as well. The buzz in the room went quiet with the director's call for silence. Then came the order "Action!" and the cameras started to roll. Only seconds had gone by when the quiet in the room was broken by the sound of loud footsteps directly overhead. Someone upstairs had not taken the director's order to heart.

The take was cut before it began, while the director demanded to know who was up there, ruining his shot. Marge and several of the crew ran upstairs to investigate. The hall was dark and empty. They went to Room 7, located directly over the bar. Marge unlocked the door and switched on the light, which only illuminated an empty room.

The movement above the bar did not end with this incident. While the footfalls were not nearly so loud again, there was an almost constant creaking, a light-footed pacing treading back and forth upstairs. The film crew settled in to focus on the job at hand. But Marge was always conscious of the pacing, deciding that whatever was up there was unhappy that so many people were crowded into the bar in the winter, a time when the hotel was usually empty.

And the presence in the hotel did not settle down immediately after the crew left. Curator Pat Roth stopped by early on the morning after the film shoot ended to clean up after the crew. She heard the footfalls even before she stepped inside—a loud and determined stride, cowboy boots walking up and down a wooden hallway. At a loss as to who could be inside the hotel, she walked in cautiously, following the sound of the footsteps to the hallway on the main floor. The footfalls persisted, even as she was standing there looking at an empty hall; no one was in sight. Up and down the hall, the agitated sound of cowboy boots on the wooden floor continued, yet there was no one there, and the hallway was carpeted.

Profoundly unsettled, Pat went about her work as quickly as she could, with the footfalls continuing the entire time. The job took her an hour, and she was glad when she was finally able to leave and lock the door behind her. When she returned later that morning to pick up some chairs from the bar, the boots were still clomping up and down the hall in their agitated tempo. She did not remain in the hotel for any longer than she needed to.

For whatever reason, the intrusion of so many people in the middle of winter stirred up the presence. When Marge returned later that day, the fretful pacing in the hall still had not abated. There to do a final inventory, she was overcome by an undeniable sense that she was not welcome. The entire time she was looking over the bar, she felt that the invisible pacer in the hall was saying something to her. His message was not audible, but she could hear it nevertheless, over and over in her mind, telling her to get out. There was no way to convince the presence in the hall that she meant no harm by being there, so she hurried to comply, finishing her work and leaving the hotel as soon as she could.

By all accounts, this was the most dramatic spiritual manifestation to occur in the Nevada City Hotel, if not the whole ghost town. No one can say for certain who the spirit is; the turbulent history of Nevada City certainly allows for it to be one of any number of its former residents. Those people hoping to keep the number of restless spirits down to as low a number as possible like to believe that the footsteps heard outside of Cabin 5 are the same as those in the Nevada City Hotel. It is true that both phenomena have manifested in the exact same way, but of course, no one can say for sure if they are the same or not.

It has also been suggested that these footsteps may belong to Charlie Bovey. Certainly the ghost town's sponsor loved it enough to continue visiting in the afterlife. Perhaps the slow footsteps heard on the boardwalk outside of Cabin 5 do indeed belong to Bovey, who carefully makes the rounds on certain winter nights, making sure that everything is in order. But then it is also said that Charlie Bovey did not wear cowboy boots, so unless he developed a new liking for the footwear in the afterlife, there is at least one good argument against this theory.

Whatever the case, it is generally refuted that the footfalls in the hotel could have belonged to Bovey. For he was always a congenial and welcoming man, and he would have been far more hospitable to any large group of visitors to the hotel, no matter what time of year. Of course, the woman in Room 12 and the spirit belonging to the disembodied cowboy boots are not coming forward with any information to clear up the matter. Thus, as is usually the case with supernatural phenomena, the occurrences in Nevada City leave little but unanswered questions in their wake.

4
Wild
Montana

The Chase in the Woods

"I definitely wouldn't call myself the kind of guy who scares easy," says Rich, who agrees to tell his story on condition of anonymity. "I've always been into watching scary movies and Stephen King is one of my favorite guys to read, but I never took any of that stuff to heart—none of it ever really stuck. I've got friends who went and saw *The Ring* or *The Others* and were going on about how much it freaked them out. Me and my girlfriend went to see *Blair Witch* together when it was out in theaters, and she was having issues shutting out the lights to go to sleep for a few nights after that, if you can believe it." Rich claims that as much as he enjoys the stories of the horror genre, he finds it easy to walk away from them.

In fact, he has never considered the possibility that there might be some truth to anything in the genre. Certainly, most rational individuals would agree. "Seriously, Freddy Kruger, Jason, killer clowns, houses built over old Indian burial grounds—fun stuff," Rich says, "but not the kind of thing you should be taking too seriously."

A horror genre aficionado who was nevertheless a staunch skeptic when it came to supernatural matters, Rich had an experience that changed his outlook during a camping trip to Montana in the summer of 2002. A self-described outdoors enthusiast, Rich has long been in the habit of taking several camping trips into the mountains every summer.

"I'm from Calgary, you know, right on the Rockies' doorstep," he says. "It's hard to grow up in a place like this and not be into the outdoors. When I was a kid, I thought the trees, exercise and clean air were good and all, but it was the nights out there that were my favorite part, sitting around the fire, roasting marshmallows by some creek while my dad or uncle would spin some gruesome story about a serial killer or a monster or a ghost. Even though you never believed them, something always happened when we called it a night and got into our sleeping bags. Sleeping outdoors like that always made my imagination go haywire. Suddenly all those stories that were totally unbelievable before didn't seem that way anymore, and every sound out there made you jump. Those nights were scary fun in a way that no horror movie or book could be." Of course, Rich was not the only youngster to get caught up in the thrill of a good campfire ghost story, but that thrill inevitably faded as he got older. One night in Lewis and Clark National Park brought that old thrill back with a vengeance.

"I went down with three of my buddies," he begins. "We'd been camping around Calgary for so long and thought maybe it would be good to make the trip down, just for a change. We didn't really plan the whole thing so much, just cleared up an extra long weekend, packed up our gear and our bikes and headed south. West Montana was the destination, but that was about as specific as it got. Other than that, we had no idea where we were going to end up."

Their spontaneous route took them to the Swan Range, through a stretch of Lewis and Clark National Forest in Teton County. "We ended up camping where we did just because we didn't know where else to go. It was getting dark and there we were, on a turnoff to a campsite—so we took it." So the site they had chosen was out of necessity more than anything else, but Rich claims he had a strange feeling about it from the onset.

"It was beautiful country we stumbled on, there's no question about that, but there was something about the campsite that felt wrong." As sure as he was about this feeling, Rich has problems articulating it to this day. "I don't know how to describe it without sounding like a total flake," he says, "but it was just in the air. There was no one around, and it was this really bare site—no showers, no running water, no fire pit. Just this clearing in the woods that you could drive up to. As far as I could tell, the only other person there besides us was the site supervisor, who lived in his trailer about half an hour by car from where we were at."

But it was not just the sense of isolation to the place. "I'd been in a lot of out of the way places before, and I'd never had any problems with that," he says. "It was something about the site, those woods. There was a feeling that the shadows were looking at us or something. It was so quiet, too. I couldn't stop thinking that the quiet was on account of something holding its breath." Rich sensed that the woods did not want them there, and he was not shy sharing this premonition with his friends.

"That didn't go over too well. It was all the predictable stuff. They had a good laugh about it. Really, that kind of thing was way too far fetched for these guys to take seriously. Not that I can really blame them or anything, either. It was pretty out there, and it was getting late and we all just wanted to set up camp and have some food already."

So Rich did his best to ignore the unsettling feeling in the back of his mind and went ahead and helped set up camp. That night, the four men sat around the small fire and did everything they could to ignore the growing unease. "Yeah, we weren't talking about it, except to crack jokes," Rich says. "No one was ready to let what I said about the place go, and there was a lot of 'What was that? You hear that?' and, 'I just saw someone out there!' We were all having a good laugh over it, that's for sure, but as it got darker and darker, it was pretty obvious that we were all nervous about it. It really was creepy out there, and I think the wisecracks were a way of dealing with it."

Rich pauses for a long moment when he is asked how, exactly, things were getting creepy. "If I go on about the lead-up to what actually happened, I'm going to sound like a flake again," he says. "Who knows? Could be that all it takes for a place to feel strange is for one person to say: 'Doesn't this place feel strange?' and then everyone's imagination does the rest. But something about that place definitely felt strange." And according to Rich, as more and more stars blinked into sight, it began to feel stranger and stranger—though neither Rich nor his friends were quite ready to acknowledge it.

Everyone who has ever been out camping is aware of what happens in the woods when the sun goes down: the shuffling of nocturnal creatures, the rustling of branches and the occasional bestial grunt or cry. The soundscape has a way of rattling people with overactive imaginations, and, perhaps, even those with very little imagination.

Rich continues, "Well, all those things that go bump in the night were really going it at it. It was all well and good to kid about it at first, but the lower that fire got, the less laughter you heard."

Rich says that it was sometime past 10:00 PM when the first genuinely concerned "What was that?" was uttered. "The crazy thing was that we all heard it, too. It was this weird low, gurgling sound that frankly freaked me right out." He explains that there was nothing very threatening in the sound in itself, but in all his years of camping, he had never heard an animal make such a sound. And there was also the fact that it sounded vaguely human.

"It didn't last for any more than a few seconds," he says, "but, boy, did it really set the tone for the rest of the night. Let's just say there wasn't too much laughing after that." No laughter, but, according to Rich, a long, stunned silence followed by hushed speculation as to what the noise could have been. "No one was getting into how freaked out they were. We started listing every animal we could think of. Kind of like 'What do they have down here in Montana that we don't?' " No one could come up with any satisfactory answers.

"It was definitely a bizarre situation," Rich says. "The thing we heard was definitely weird, but it was also a tough thing sitting there trying to come up with something— anything to say about it. Because looking back, that was the most important thing, I think. We had to keep talking."

And they continued to do so as new sounds came out of the darkness. "Maybe about 10 or 15 minutes after that gurgling, the snapping began," he says. "It was like there was someone out there, maybe 20 or 30 feet away, breaking small branches off the trees and piling them up right near the edge of our clearing. It came with this shuffling, too, like something moving back and forth to this pile of branches it was making." Rich says they all heard the sound of the mounting pile, as well. The falling and stacking of branches, one at a time, suggested that whatever was out there, it was industrious.

But what was it working toward? "At that point, we started asking questions. You know—'Hello? Is anybody there?' That kind of stuff." They received no reply, and none of them felt like walking out and taking a look at what was going on, so they settled on the best explanation: it was a beaver. Rich laughs. "I think it just got to the point where no one was willing to take a look, and we had to get to bed. We just told ourselves something that would make it easier to call it a night. Because how long could we sit around there and scare ourselves to death? So, sure, it's a beaver? It has to be a beaver mucking around with tree branches near our site. Better that than a crazy person with an ax or, God knows, whatever else it might be."

The coping mechanism had worked well enough in getting them into their tents, but it did little for Rich when he woke from sleep later on that night. "The worst thing in the world about camping is when you've got to go to the washroom in the middle night. You know—you've got to get out of your sleeping bag, get out of the tent, dig for your shoes, find the outhouse. I usually don't even bother unless I *really* have to go."

This was one of those times. Groggily, Rich crawled from his sleeping bag. Fumbling with his flashlight and stumbling from his tent with shoes untied, he took a moment to allow his eyes to adjust before heading for the outhouse. In his half-conscious state, he was not thinking about the unsettling noises from the trees. "I don't think there's anybody who's walked through the woods at night and thought, 'Ho-Hum, isn't this nice.' It's just the simple truth that there's something creepy about being in the

"It's just the simple truth that there's something creepy about being in the woods at night."

woods at night. You can't help it. Sure, you're not going to get hysterical, but I don't care who you are, if it's nighttime and you're in the woods by yourself, there's a small part of you that isn't happy about it. Maybe we inherited it from our ancestors—that part of us that's still coping with being chased around by saber-toothed tigers."

Rich, the lifetime camper that he is, claims to have gotten over his fear of the sylvan dark—mostly. With just a trace of unease, Rich navigated the trail through the trees, lighting his way with the flashlight in his hand. "I was doing fine, I think, until I was about halfway to the outhouse, and that damn beaver started stacking wood again." The sound of stacking branches seemed louder, nearer now than it had been before. Until then, Rich had not given any thought to the sounds they had heard earlier that night.

"It was a lot easier to buy this ridiculous explanation of a beaver when you're sitting there with three other guys who are willing to believe the same thing. It changes when you're out there by yourself, though, and you come face-to-face with the fact that there's just no possible way that could be true—there's something out there, and I've got no idea what it is."

Rich continued to the outhouse. "I was spooked at that point, but not enough to forget my bladder—I just picked up the pace and ignored my butterflies." But those butterflies became hornets when a sudden rustling sounded from the darkness. "It came from the bush along the trail; something was moving out there, and it sounded close— maybe like 10 or 15 yards away, 20 tops."

The question became pressing then: continue to the outhouse, or turn around and run for the campsite? Rich says his fear at the time was very real, but it was still not so big that he could forget his reason for being out there in the first place—he still had to go to the washroom. Going back to the wildlife theory, he imagined that he heard the sound of voles, raccoons and other nocturnal creatures, and he continued on his way.

"Everything that happened that night's been burned into my head, but the time frame's a bit muddy," says Rich. "I can't say for sure if it was a few seconds or a few minutes after that when the gargling started up. All I can say for sure is that it happened before I got to the outhouse. I remember hearing it, I think, at the exact same time I saw the outhouse." And that was the very moment that Rich panicked.

"That was it," he says. "There wasn't too much thinking after that. The legs took over at that point, and they were all about taking me out of there right quick." It amounted to a headlong run into the darkness. "What hit me hardest was how close it was—that and the feeling that whatever this thing was, I was completely sure that it was following me."

Without another thought, he was running flat out through the woods, tenuously guided by his wildly wobbling flashlight. "I was totally freaked out at that point," he says. "But as soon as I started running, I knew that whatever I heard sped up, too." He could hear it crashing through the trees next to the trail—the footfalls on the leaves, the gargling grunts in the darkness.

"It's a little mixed up when I think about it now," he says. "I remember thinking that it was catching up to me, but I can't remember exactly why I had that feeling. It wasn't like I heard it getting closer. And there was no way I was turning around to take a look, so I couldn't see it gaining. But I felt it in my gut. Whatever was out there was way faster than I was, and it was coming up quick. I was sure of it. I could feel it in my chest, and let me tell you, I don't think I've ever been so scared."

Panic came over him, and Rich was running blind, dashing over root and rock, sure that there was something behind him, right at his heels, but he was too scared to turn around and look. All he knew was that he had to run; it was the only clear thought that made it through the panic.

"One thing's for sure, I know what people mean by panic attack," Rich says. "I think it was only about one minute, two tops, where I wasn't thinking straight at all, and I ended up taking a wrong turn on the way back. Suddenly, there was no trail at all and I hit this root and went down."

Rich hit the ground hard, landing on his stomach and gasping for breath as the air rushed from him. "I was trying to shout but couldn't get anything out because I was winded. Then the scariest thing happened. The best way I can describe it is to say it was a wave of cold that moved over me, starting at my feet and moving up, over my back and neck and up to my head. I could feel goosebumps moving up with the cold, and when it got up to my head, it felt like my hair was standing straight up, like the way scared people look in cartoons."

Without a mirror, Rich had no way of knowing if this was actually the case, but in that moment, he was far too scared to give the matter any thought. Every hair on his head may well have been turning white as he turned over to face the thing he was certain was standing over him.

On his back, propped up on his elbows, Rich looked up, and what he saw filled him with wonder and terror.

"There was this shape, like the shape of a man surrounded by a dense, heavy mist that was giving off this low, silvery light. It was like this small cloud that was swirling all around a man inside. The mist made it hard to make out any details, but I could see that he was tall, over six feet, with big shoulders. That was all."

Rich cannot say for certain how long he lay there, looking in wonder at the apparition before him, but it took a couple of minutes, at least, before he was able to find his voice. "Yeah, for the first little bit, all I could do was stare," he says. "I don't know if I was so much scared as just totally shocked—if that makes sense. At one point, I was trying to say, 'What are you?' but my mouth couldn't get around the words. All I managed to get out was a stuttering babble. This thing had me cold all over, and it was like my mouth froze up, too."

But Rich eventually found his voice. "I took a few deep breaths, pulled myself together and finally asked what on earth it was." What happened next shocked Rich as much as the apparition's first appearance.

"I don't think I was really expecting this thing to answer me," he says. "It looked like a man, sure, but there was no way I was mistaking this thing for anything human. Who knew if it could even speak?" Given what he had already gone through that night—lying on the ground, staring up at a silhouette enshrouded in glowing mist—Rich was beyond shock or surprise. But there was more to come.

"The only answer I got was that ugly gargling sound we'd been hearing all night," Rich says, "but the thing on the trail wasn't what made the sound." In fact, according to Rich, the apparition heard it as clearly as he did, and by his account, it was not at all happy about it. "The thing swung its head around and looked over its shoulder and then shot off past me and into the woods," he says. "Right after that, there was this crashing in the bush and something else moved past me. I couldn't see it because it was in the trees, but I could tell that it was moving fast. There was something else out there, and it was going after the thing that went after me. It was a chase."

Thus, Rich's encounter in the woods went from freakish to completely incomprehensible. Yet he did not waste any time lying around trying to find answers. "As soon as those two went by, I was back on my feet," he says. "I was running back to the campsite double quick."

Lying in his tent, Rich did not sleep at all for the rest of the night, and when the topic of the gargling noise came up at breakfast the next morning, he said nothing of his experiences the night before. "I've talked about it with some people since then," he says, "but never with the guys I camp with. It would have been some big joke or something." And while Rich makes it clear that he usually has no problems with his camping friends' brand of humor, he did not want them to make fun of what he experienced that night. "Anyway," he continues, "how do you tell a gang of hard-nosed guys that you got chased by a ghost?" Rich's answer's simple: you don't.

Beyond that, Rich is decidedly short on answers regarding what happened that night in the woods of Teton County. "I've thought about it over and over until I've driven myself half crazy," he says. "I still have no idea what I saw out there, and what chased it away." He has a few theories, and brings up the possibility of Native spirits, followed by an idea of his own, where the glowing figure is the ghost of a hunter, and the crashing in the trees was a supernatural manifestation of its long-dead quarry. "Maybe he was chasing me because he mistook me for what he was hunting, but realized his mistake when he heard the gargling sound in the trees."

When asked what sort of creature this ghostly hunter may have been after, Rich freely admits the limitations of his theory. "I have no idea," he says.

It has been a number of years since Rich's encounter in the woods, and though he admits that he still finds himself dwelling on what happened that night, he has learned to be content with not knowing.

"There are some things that, no matter how much we study, or how far we advance, we'll never understand. I know that now. That night in the woods changed my life."

The Vision at Lake McDonald

Montana is an outdoorsman's state. In its arid eastern plains rising to the rugged alpine of the Rocky Mountains, its ranches, farms, parks and incredible natural beauty, there is something of the imagined "frontier" that still lives, and not just in the ghost towns and abandoned mines that dot the countryside and the old Victorian homes that line the more distinguished streets of its cities. Some part of the past lives on in the outdoors, in the forests and the lakes, among the rocky crags. The land itself can seem haunted, appearing, in certain locations and at certain times, like the ghost of an America that once was but now is lost.

There are some people who are all too aware of the ghost of this bygone America. They seek it out among the trails in the Cabinet Mountains, in Glacier National Park campsites and in the way the night sky stretches over an alpine lake framed by rocky peaks. The spirit in these places is quiet, unrushed, unpretentious, uninvolved. People seek it out, even run to it, when the pace of the world drums its maddening cadence in their veins and they have forgotten how to slow down.

"I was a younger man when we used to take our trips to Glacier National Park," says Lionel Adam. "The less I say about myself, the better, but if you met me in everyday life, I don't think I'd be the kind of guy you'd guess would believe in ghosts. I'll just say that I work with my hands and don't usually believe in anything I can't fix with a wrench."

That said, Adam admits he has long had an appreciation for the outdoors—an appreciation that, when pressed,
he has difficulty explaining. "It was in my family when we
were growing up. My dad used to take me and my brother
camping, like anyone else, I guess. But nothing about it
stuck with my brother. He moved out East as soon as he
got out of school and doesn't come back much. Me, I don't
think I'd ever want to be so far away from the mountains. I
need to see them, from time to time, at least."

Still, Adam does not see them as much as he used to. "A
man my age isn't going to get out as much as he used to,"
he says. "Back when I was younger, though, and the kids
were still around, we'd make it out as much as we could.
Usually there'd be three or four trips out camping somewhere in the summer. I made sure of it."

He admits there was a slight problem with these outings, especially when his children got older and were no
longer so eager to spend stretches of their summer holidays roasting wieners with their parents. "A man might
love doing something more than anything else, but that
doesn't mean his family's going to feel the same way. A difference like that can really affect you, too, if you let it. Took
me a while to learn it, but I figure you're better off if you
let people be who they are."

Adam's family grew tired of camping long before his
passion for it waned, a fact that he was not happy about.
"Early on, me and my wife used to do a lot of it. Had a little tradition for a few years to drive down to Yellowstone,
as far south as Utah. That was before the kids showed up.
After that, we usually didn't drive out too far. I was surprised how quickly my wife got sick of it when the kids
stopped coming. I guess I thought we'd keep doing it

ourselves, but that didn't happen. When the kids stopped, we all stopped. I never liked the idea of going out there on my own, and I only made it out after that when I got around to planning it with some friends. That wasn't much."

But when they did go, one of their favorite destinations was the expansive Glacier National Park, on the Canadian border. "I guess it was mostly in my head, but I always got the feeling that things really clicked with us all when we were there. I know I was extra relaxed, and the kids weren't at each other's throats all the time. Or so I thought, anyway. My wife told me later that those trips to Glacier were for me more than anyone else. She and the kids played along just because it meant a lot to me. That's what she told me, anyway."

As much as he appreciated all the park's landmarks, Adam was especially taken with Lake McDonald. "Don't ask me why," he says. "I could sit there by that lake for hours. It always felt more like home to me than home did. My wife used to kid around about how I was probably an Indian or something in a past life. Who knows, she could be right." Certainly the thing that happened on one of the last times he made the trip to the park with his family convinced Adam that he did, in fact, have a bond with the place. The nature of the bond, however, he could only guess at.

"That was early August, when we made that trip," he says. "I took some time off work and made a long weekend out of it. We drove up and got there sometime past noon and set up camp close to the lake. We got lucky and found one of my favorite spots—close enough to the lake to see it easy, but we were in the woods. Nice and quiet."

The camping trip began like any other. Adam admits he does not trust his memories of those excursions as well as he once did, having been told a number of times since then that they were not as idyllic as he remembered them to be. Still, he insists that things began to change as the sun began to set, in very subtle ways.

"Back then, we were having some problems with our daughter," he says. "They weren't big problems when I think about them now—normal things teenagers deal with. But when it was going on, we were worried. We weren't crazy about the friends she was running with, and her marks weren't what they used to be." While Adam says he was just as concerned about their daughter as his wife was, he managed to keep things civil with his child. His wife, on the other hand, had taken to having regular arguments with her, and the whole family had gotten used to a constant tension when mother and daughter were in the same room. According to Adam, however, on that summer evening, his wife and daughter were getting along as the sun sank beneath the tree line.

Daughter and mother exchanged healthy banter as Adam's son, a rather bookish teenager who, by this time, would rather be reading than throwing himself into campsite tasks, helped his father with the fire. "There was a really good thing going on," he says. "I'm saying that my wife and daughter started singing while they were putting dinner together. It was just plain weird."

Even with the unhappiest of families, there can be moments of reprieve, when issues are shed for a happy instant or two. That night, camped near Lake McDonald in Montana's popular national park, Adam's family enjoyed just such a time as the antagonisms and differences that had slowly taken root among them dissolved—for a night at least. For Adam, it was a validation of his passion for the outdoors, of his underlying philosophy that it is the pressures of the contemporary world, the rush and expectations of daily life, that alienate one from the other. On this trip, however, he came to believe something else about the outdoors—that there were forces at work, forces with a very human face.

"I think I started to get the feeling sometime after my wife and I were walking back to our campsite from the lake. We went down there to get a little time away from the kids, watch the sky change color and all that." After about 10 or 15 minutes down by the lake, the couple began to walk back to their campsite. That was when Adam sensed it for the first time.

"I can tell you for sure that it was footsteps in the bush, moving just behind us," Adam says. "Not heavy steps either, but real light and careful. It wasn't an animal in there, but someone picking their steps." Turning immediately to the sound of the footfalls, he saw a vaguely human shape in the shadows, only visible for a few moments before blending in with the surrounding darkness.

"Well, I spooked my wife out good and proper," he says. "I froze on the spot and shone my flashlight into the bush, and she had no idea what was going on. She hadn't heard anything." The questions began immediately, as his now anxious wife demanded to know what he had stopped for. Not wanting to alarm his wife, Adam downplayed the event. "I told her it was nothing, that I thought I heard something, but it was probably just a bird or something."

The attempt to put his wife's mind at ease was not entirely successful, especially after Adam heard the footsteps resume when he and his wife began walking again. This time he deliberated the matter. Realizing that stopping and shining his light into the bush would alarm his wife all the more, and not wanting to ruin what had been an excellent evening, he decided to do his best to ignore the sound and continue on. The problem was that he was not doing such a great job at the ignoring part.

"I couldn't believe my wife didn't hear it. Like I said, it wasn't stomping around in there, but it was definitely loud enough to hear—for me anyway, it was fairly obvious. But my wife had no clue." While she was unaware of the faint footsteps he was hearing, Adam's wife was definitely in tune with her husband, and she could tell that there was something wrong.

"She said something like, 'I'm going to scream if you look over your shoulder one more time, man.' I tried to laugh it off. I asked her if she didn't hear those steps, or if I was losing my mind. But she wasn't hearing anything and said it was probably true that I'd lost my mind a long time ago." Doing his best to put on a nonchalant face, Adam did not stop again until they had reached their campsite, though he was conscious of the presence the entire way.

"When we got back, my wife made a crack about how there was an ax-murdering rabbit on our tail." Adam laughed along with his children but quickly excused himself, telling his family that he wanted to get a look at what "furry little creature" had followed them up from the lake. "I don't think they thought too much about that," he says. "We'd all spent a lot of time camping, and there are a lot of animals you'll see in the bush. I think it was sort of weird that I'd take the time out to go after a vole or

Lake McDonald

something. But then the old man's strange anyway, and who pays attention to him anyway, right?"

So Adam strode back out into the bush, doing his best to ignore the cold feeling that was beginning to creep up his back—the very real sense that this was no nocturnal mammal he was going after. "There was something in the bush," he says. "I didn't know what it was, but I knew it wasn't a vole."

Heading out into the darkness with a flashlight and a certainty that someone, or something, lurked there—wasn't Adam frightened? "That's one of the craziest things about it all," he replies. "I think I should have been scared about what was going on, but there wasn't any fear. It was actually more like excitement. Like there was something no one had ever seen before in those woods—proof of the Almighty or the Bigfoot or I don't know what else. I can't remember the last time my heart was going like that. Maybe when I was a kid on Christmas morning."

Led by the narrow beam of his flashlight, Adam was conscious of little else besides his eagerness and the thing that he was sure lurked just beyond his sight in the darkness that enveloped him. "The gut feeling was turned right around when I went into those trees," he says. "I wasn't being followed anymore. It wasn't coming after me. I was going after it—and I'm telling you, that made a big difference."

Now Adam was the one doing the stalking. Above his clumsy steps, he could hear the sound of the faint retreat; the footsteps that had come after him and his wife were now retreating deeper into the woods, back toward the lake. "I was bent on it going after it, but I can't really say why," Adam continues. "I just had this itch way down deep telling me there was something in those trees that no one had ever seen before, and I was going to find out what."

This enthusiasm took him on a path he is no longer able to recall, through alpine bush, over roots and around trees, stumbling on the uneven ground. "That little jaunt down to the lake happened a long time ago," he says, "but sometimes I wonder if it happened at all." Adam makes it clear that he has always prided himself on a being a "steady thinker," not prone to fits of passion or unpredictable behavior. "What you see is what you get," he says. "I'm not the sort to flake out and get dramatic over anything." In short, running headlong through the trees in the darkness after footsteps only he could hear was highly unusual for him.

"I don't know how long I walked, but I ended up back at the lake." Adam describes a striking scene—the water as still as glass, reflecting the starry sky and surrounding mountain peaks. "It was a spectacular sight," he says. "I'm saying it was so incredible that I think there was a second or two where I forgot what I was doing down there in the first place." Then he spied movement on the water, and the frisson of expectation came back.

"I pointed my light at the water, but the beam wasn't strong enough; it just made everything black." Yet when Adam turned his light away from the lake and let his eyes adjust to the starlit night, the dim silhouette appeared again. "It was a really faint outline," he says. "It was really black out there, and the shape I was looking at wasn't close, either. By all rights, it should have been underwater, but it was standing on top of the water, just standing there looking back at me."

Or that is what he suspected, anyway. When asked how he can be certain that a figure he could barely see was looking at him, Adam resorts back to talk about strong hunches. "For starters, I was the only person out there," he says. "Who else would it be looking at? And the longer I stood there, the clearer it became. It was partly my eyes getting used to the dark, but there was also something else going on. A light started to shine out there on the water."

Staring transfixed, Adam was able to make out more and more of the figure on the lake as the dim light shone brighter with each passing second. It was at this point that Adam's attitude about the goings-on began to change. He laughs about this abrupt change when he talks about it today. "Go figure. Now that I was looking at something that no one had ever seen before, I wasn't sure if I wanted to be seeing it." The excitement that, until then, had been motivating him suddenly turned into something that resembled fear.

"I'm sure it sounds crazy as anything," he says. "Here I am chasing these footsteps down to the lake, eager as a kid on his birthday. But then when I can see what I'm going after, I've got to get the hell away from it. Makes sense, right?" Comprehensible or not, the fear came on strong, and our normally stoic, level-headed eyewitness found himself wrestling with the new emotion.

"What did I do?" Adam laughs. "I got myself out of there—that's what. Footsteps in the forest got me all eager, sure. Seeing it out there on the water changed everything, though. I didn't know what to do next. And out there on the water, it didn't look like it was making any suggestions, either." Then Adam adds one more detail, which seems to be the deciding factor. "Also, it wasn't an it. It was a woman."

The apparition was gleaming in a monochrome silver light, "like if you took the moon minus a few watts," as Adam describes it. There were no discernable features where its face was, but Adam could clearly see that it was a woman, with a long sheet of silver hair and an unmistakably female silhouette.

Speaking about it today, he does not know why this fact threw him the way it did. Perhaps the fact that the mystical force that had guided him was gendered was so unexpected that he reacted with fear. Or maybe it was just that the sight of it, shining with dim opalescence out on the lake, was simply too much to digest.

"I pretty well panicked. I turned around and ran the other way. Went a bit too fast, too. I had no idea where I was putting my feet, and I ended up falling over a bunch of times." Thankfully, for the sake of his family's peace of mind, Adam's panic did not last. Calming down after he put some distance between himself and the lake, he stopped to take stock of the situation. This was no easy thing.

"That was the first time I stopped and said, 'What is going on here?' This thing was getting under my skin, making me crazy, running around this campground in the middle of the night. I was having trouble making sense of it—didn't even know for sure if I was thrilled or spooked about it. There were a few seconds where I thought maybe I was going crazy."

Deciding that he was best off being around what was familiar, Adam began walking back to his family. "There I was, thinking that they'd be worried sick about where I'd gone," he says. "It turns out the kids were barely interested. Who knows what they were thinking, but it didn't have anything to do with me. My son was reading by the fire; my daughter and my wife were playing cards."

Although his children were not interested, his wife noticed that something was wrong. She looked at him carefully before gesturing to the dirt on his clothes and asking him what he had been up to. "I made a joke about how I'd been out wrestling with a Bigfoot," Adam says. "My daughter asked me who won, and they had a bit of a laugh." Adam had no intention of telling them what he had seen, but his wife continued to press the matter. "I could tell she knew something was up, and she wasn't just going to let it go."

Adam's wife asked him if he had any luck tracking down the thing he had heard. "I told her 'no.' All I got for my troubles was a few spills and sore knees. I also told her that I made it down to the lake, and that it was something to see at night." But this was as far as Adam went; he said nothing of the female apparition hovering over the water.

Content to do no more investigating into the matter of what, exactly, was out there, Adam settled down by the fire and tried to engage his uninterested son in conversation. His efforts did not get him far, but as Adam began to unwind among the familiar personalities of his family, an odd thing happened. "It's another tough one to explain," he says, "but it was like I was looking around at my family with new eyes. I don't think I ever spent too much time thinking about the big picture—about how we're not here for too long, and we ought to appreciate what we have while we still have it."

Adam's thoughts turned to the woman on the water, and he wondered why she might have followed him and his wife to their campsite. He thought about being alone on cold and beautiful Lake McDonald. "Out of nowhere, I felt bad for that woman out on the lake and really grateful for the family I had. Sure, I was invisible to them half the time, but then maybe that's a sign that I'm doing my job, right? As far as I'm concerned, no drama out of Dad is a good thing."

But there would be just a little more drama before that night was over. The ghostly woman returned when the fire was down to embers. The campers' breath billowed before them in the cold alpine night, and it was time for bed. It had been a quiet night, but a night that Adam had been grateful for. "My son was the first to call it a night, and the rest of us followed after that." Right behind his wife, Adam was the last one to crawl into his tent. Just before he did, he cast one look over his shoulder. And there she was.

"She was standing in the trees, right at the edge of our campsite. She looked like she did on the lake, glowing all silver-like, but now her face was as clear as day. I can't really say how old she was; she wasn't young, but she wasn't old either. I've always had problems remembering her face after she disappeared, but what I couldn't forget was the way she was looking at me. She had a kind, happy expression on her face. As weird as it was to have this glowing woman standing there, watching us, I know she didn't mean harm. It's plain crazy, I know, but after that night, I've always had this feeling that she was looking at us and thinking how lucky we were. Could be she was lonely or something. She missed her family and was happy to see another one."

Adam's wife, however, did not share this optimistic interpretation. "I didn't tell her about it for a few more days. She really didn't like it, me talking about a glowing woman floating over a lake and following us around in the woods. It got a lot harder to get her out camping after that—not that it was ever that easy to begin with."

To this day, Adam does not know if his wife was bothered by her dependably straightforward husband's uncharacteristic behavior, coming up with such a bizarre story and trying to pass it off as the truth, or if she was more concerned about the possibility that his bizarre story might actually be the truth. If so, she was obviously uneasy about the notion of an unknown shining woman—kindly or not—watching her and her family in the wilderness.

For his part, Adam still does not know what to make of what he saw. "Some days I think about the whole thing and wonder if I might have gone temporarily crazy or who knows what else. Those had been tough days for both of us. We had teenagers and a lot of debt and didn't know what to make of the future. Who knows—it could be the strain got to me." But then Adam says that he is usually quite certain that he was not hallucinating, that, for whatever reason, there really had been a silver woman who lured him to the lake and inspired in him a newfound appreciation for his family. "At church we're always hearing about how there are forces bigger than us that are working in ways we can't understand. Well, I guess you could say that after that night all those years back, I'm more inclined to believe it."

Montana's Earth Lights

Sometime in the 1920s, on a homestead near Grass Range, Fergus County, a boy woke up in the middle of the night, his eyes fixed on a faint glow in his window. He had woken like this before, anxious and excited in the deep hours of the night, mesmerized by the mystery hovering outside on the prairie. Getting out of bed, he slowly walked over the creaking floorboards to the window. The light looked the same as it always had, a white circle swinging slightly, as though someone was carrying a lantern out there, across the field. But the boy, like every one of the surrounding homesteaders who had seen the light, knew this was not the case. The light had been appearing for years now, and people said that a lot of men went after it, but not one ever returned with a lantern or even a hint as to who might have been carrying it. Their reports always amounted to the same thing: the light simply vanished. It was there, and then it was gone.

In the past, the boy had always been content to watch the light from his bedroom window, to stand there in silence and dwell on its mystery. But there was something different about tonight. An unseasonable warmth hung in the early fall air; the final remnants of a summer restlessness blew on a fitful wind. The bobbing glow, usually so apart, so removed from any part of the boy's daily life on the homestead, tonight seemed to beckon to him. When it had appeared before, it had always looked too far away, impossible to catch. On this night, however, it seemed as though it might be close—within reach of a good run, perhaps just a few hundred yards away. The boy decided to go after it.

Careful not to wake his parents, the boy slipped on a shirt and pants, tied up his boots at the front door and crept out into the night. The light was hovering there still. It seemed even closer than before, and he began walking toward it quickly, eager to uncover the mystery that had long baffled the cluster of homesteads.

The light had first been spotted over a decade ago by a neighboring homesteader who had been out on his land toiling late into the night. The story goes that this man did not make much of it, assuming that it was the local moonshiner making a nightly delivery. Repeated sightings in the following weeks made it clear that the moonshiner had nothing to do with the bobbing light, and that something strange was going on.

Subsequent sightings had the light changing shape and color. Some homesteaders described a small pinpoint appearing to be at a great distance, oscillating in weird patterns near the horizon. Others perceived the light as being much closer, a big orb hovering over their farmland, swaying as it approached and then receded in erratic patterns, as though it were a lantern held by a lost and lurching drunk.

There was more than one homesteader who, believing the light to be close, set out after it, intent on uncovering the mystery once and for all. These men's experiences, stumbling through the darkness in pursuit of the glowing orb, disproved the notion that the resident bootlegger was running regular deliveries at night. The chases yielded such bizarre stories that many who were involved began to wonder if they were going after something that could not be caught—if whoever, or, more likely, whatever, was out there was not human. Perhaps there was no one there holding the light. Maybe the light was it. But what was it? The stories of the chases spread through the community, and it was not long before everyone was asking this question.

Some of the men spoke of the light growing larger with every step, giving them the impression that they were drawing closer. Yet when any of these men called out, inquiring who was there, something unexpected would usually happen. Sometimes the light would suddenly change color, often going from white or yellow to startling crimson before vanishing altogether. On other occasions, the light would simply blink out of sight, leaving the man standing there uneasily in the darkness, thinking that whoever was carrying the lantern snuffed it out at the challenge. But in these cases, the light would rarely remain out of sight for longer than several seconds before flashing back into sight at an impossible distance that no man could realistically cover. Not even the most determined men found any trace of footprints where the light had appeared.

Years went by and the light continued to appear, usually in the fall, winter and spring, usually sometime between nine in the evening and midnight, but often later. Some of the local homesteaders grew comfortable with the mysterious apparition, while others were unable to accept it, ascribing it to evil forces. It was not uncommon to hear a solitary rifle report after sunset—the panicked reaction of a fearful man who spotted the light floating over his property.

Our own witness, however, the boy woken from sleep in the opening of our story, did not have the luxury of a firearm. The only thing he carried was his lantern, lighting the way as he walked toward the light. His parents' farmhouse quickly vanished behind him in the thick blackness of the moonless night. The world was nothing beyond the dim illumination cast by his lantern, nothing but absolute darkness and the small ball of light swinging pendulum-like in front of him.

After some time, it became difficult for the boy to gauge how far ahead the swinging light was. It had seemed close when he began, but after walking some distance, he noticed that it did not seem to be getting any closer. Then for a short while, the orb seemed to be getting larger, and he was sure he was gaining on it. When it looked as though it would be just a few minutes more—when the orb seemed so close that the light emanating from it seemed to mingle with the lantern in the boy's hand—it blinked out of sight. There had been no warning. No sound, no visual fading or flickering. It was simply there one moment, gone the next.

The boy stood frozen in the darkness for several seconds, trying to figure out what to make of the vanishing light, when it suddenly reappeared. Now, however, it was far too distant to go after; it was nothing more than an illuminated dot on the horizon. It had changed color as well, and it was now lit up like a dim, glowing red ember, somehow seeming to mock the lone boy in the field. So ended another attempt to get to the truth behind the light of Fergus County.

For the folks south of Grass Range, the mysterious light became a fact of life. Everyone had their own reactions to it. Many of the settlers living in Fergus County at the time were pragmatic people, too busy at work to bother about a solitary light appearing in the darkness. Some of the more jovial families were immensely entertained by it, setting up nocturnal picnics in the early fall with the hopes of catching sight of the swinging orb. For others, something about the appearance of the light elicited a deep and abiding fear; notions of evil spirits, anguished ghosts or an angry God colored the phenomenon in frightening shades. These people were the ones responsible for the occasional rifle reports that were heard after sunset. And finally, there were the curious—the handful of eyewitnesses who sought to understand what they were dealing with.

The first thing that these inquisitive souls would have learned is that Fergus County was not the only place where mysterious lights appeared in the middle of the night. In fact, nocturnal lights were materializing before startled farmers and ranchers just a few counties to the west. This phenomenon, however, came with a tangible explanation.

The first public mention of the lights was in an 1881 article from Helena's *Daily Herald*. The article told of a group of lights that had been appearing regularly for several months. Unlike the light in Fergus County, these luminescent orbs always materialized in the same place: on the property of the late Charles Tacke. The previous fall, Tacke had been murdered by a man named Peter Pelkey, who had promptly been found guilty and hanged for the crime. No one recalled seeing these lights while Tacke was alive, but ever since his untimely end, they had become a regular feature around the home and buildings on his property.

The conclusion was obvious. The lights were a manifestation of the restless souls of Tacke and Pelkey, unable to find peace after their violent deaths. While the explanation was generally accepted by the surrounding settlers, the reports of the phenomenon tended to differ from witness to witness. A German farmer living near the Tacke homestead spoke of the lights coming with the first snowfall. One light he described as looking like it came from a red lantern, but then it gradually changed color, turning lighter until it settled on a yellowish tinge. On some evenings, there would be only one light, but on others there were as many as four lights darting across the night sky with lively and erratic movements, rising as high as 20 feet into the air.

Another farmer described far more lethargic orbs. He first saw them in early fall. To his eyes, they were big, bright spheres moving slowly, with seeming deliberation, over the Tacke farm. These lights continued to move across the land until they reached the house and outbuildings. There, they would begin a slow orbit around the structures, rising as they circled and then rising still higher, until they were so high above the landscape that they became lost among the stars.

Yet another account has two lucid and respected observers noting the appearance of a large, floating orb while traveling a road bordering the Tacke farm. This pair reported a single sphere hovering over the land at anywhere from 10 to 40 feet in the air. These men even hazarded a guess at its proportions, estimating that it could have been a foot and a half to two feet high; they described it as lit with an orange glow for the most part, but then it would suddenly strobe to green and blue flashes.

According to the *Daily Herald* article, speculation about the lights varied widely, just as it had in Fergus County.

One theory involved a set of new-fangled electric lights that had been lifted from Edison's workshop. The more superstitious called the lights harbingers of the apocalypse. Then there was the rather bizarre, if colorful, notion that the lights had been sent from hell by the damned soul of Peter Pelkey to seek out his victim's buried money.

Although many years have passed with no further word on either of these phenomena, the inexplicable appearance of glowing spheres, commonly referred to as "earth lights," is a frequent and widespread occurrence. Indeed, earth lights have been reported so many times and in so many places over the years that they have come to be considered a legitimate type of phenomenon, complete with history, folklore and attempts at rational explanation.

Earth lights have hardly been limited to rural Montana. Observed by other peoples for centuries, they have been known by many other names. In Celtic folklore, the light that was known to appear over the bog was commonly called a will-o'-the-wisp or a Jack- o'-lantern. It was mischievous or just plain evil, luring lost or foolish travelers into dangerous terrain.

The will-o'-the-wisp is probably the best known folkloric rendition of the earth light. The legend usually involves a traveler in unfamiliar territory, walking lost without a lantern after sunset through some deserted rural landscape, usually near a bog or a precipice. The traveler is alone and feeling quite anxious about his situation when a light appears in the distance. Assuming the light to be a lantern in the hands of a fellow traveler or, better yet, a hearth fire's glow through a window, the man quickens his pace, making his way toward the light.

Buoyed by relief, he walks for some time before an uncomfortable realization begins to sink in—the light does not seem to be getting any closer. There are brief stretches where he thinks he is gaining on it, but then it somehow begins to recede, growing smaller in the darkness. He quickens his pace, determined to catch up. The sequence repeats: the light grows larger, the traveler begins to hope that he's getting closer, another moment passes and the light has regained its distance once again. He grows more determined and decides to run. Again the light draws nearer, only to rapidly recede into the darkness. He begins to get desperate. He shouts at the light, says he is lost. He needs help.

This version of the will-o'-the-wisp rarely ends well. Often the traveler is led to the edge of a dangerous cliff. While approaching the cliff, he is finally able to make out a little figure carrying a lantern, but just before he catches up with the light-bearing figure, it leaps over the edge of the precipice with a maniacal laugh, leaving the traveler alone to navigate the treacherous topography in total darkness. In other versions, he is led into the midst of a treacherous bog instead of to the edge of a cliff before the light vanishes.

The folklore differs on what the will-o'-the-wisp is. Certain versions lay the blame on faeries. Mischievous and often malevolent, these magical creatures torment for torment's sake, deriving great pleasure from misleading oafish humans. In other tales, the earth lights are restless spirits. Like the souls of Tacke and Pelkey, their manifestations are paranormal embodiments of a traumatic and premature demise. Malicious in their discontent, they act with morbid intelligence, with intentions to mislead and to harm. A

Christian interpretation of the legend makes the lights out to be the tragic souls of stillborn children, who, never having been baptized, wander over the earthly plane without cause or purpose, just as lost as the travelers they are misleading.

The Irish had their own take on the earth light, introducing the colorful story of Jack, a morally bankrupt trickster. Certain he would burn in hell for his earthly behavior, Jack came up with a plan to lure the Devil into an apple tree. Once the Devil was perched in the branches, Jack hastily carved a cross into the trunk, so that his diabolical enemy was no longer able to descend. With the Prince of Darkness completely at his mercy, Jack negotiated a deal: when he died, the Devil was not to allow him into hell. Only when he received the Devil's word that he would not burn in eternal hellfire did Jack carve out the cross and allow his captive to step down.

The plan was good, but there was one major oversight. Jack had tricked his way out of hell, but he had no scheme to con his way into heaven. When he finally passed away, Jack's manifold sins were addressed at heaven's gates, and it was promptly decided that no man as wicked as he had been would enjoy a place next to the virtuous. He was denied entry and cast down into Lucifer's sulfurous realm. But the Devil was true to his word and would not take Jack in.

Thus Jack's fate was set. Having been denied entry into heaven and tricked his way out of hell, he was cursed to remain on earth—an incorporeal spirit for eternity. The Devil did have some compassion for Jack, however, giving him a glowing ember from his burning kingdom so that he would be able to warm himself and see his way in the dark. Jack hollowed a turnip and placed the burning coal within. And the Jack-o'-lantern was born. The Irish and their descendents were wont to keep their distance from the lights that flashed in the marshes. They all knew that Jack was a bitter spirit, and he and his cursed lantern never led anyone to any good.

Not all cultures shared the negative view of earth lights. The folklore of the Finns and the Baltic states tended to look upon will-o'-the-wisps as benevolent beings, whose lights indicated the location of buried riches that could only be unearthed when the light was shining. Even among the Irish, some variations of the folktale allowed for an earth light that had the potential for kindness. For if a traveler was kind enough to be able to befriend a will-o'-the-wisp, then it might lead one away from danger rather than toward it.

But such tales, colorful as they are, tend not to be taken too seriously by the more sensible among us. These are rational times, and such wildly fanciful stories no longer hold up against rational explanation. The interesting thing about earth lights is that they have occurred widely and frequently enough to warrant attention from people with scientific sensibilities, who largely pay little mind to occurrences so readily associated with the paranormal. Yet earth lights draw crowds from Watersmeet, Michigan, to Marfa, Texas, and over a dozen places in between, making it difficult for even the most skeptical-minded to disregard them outright.

The first explanation that is often offered is that the lights are from traffic from nearby highways. Even if the cars are beyond earshot, headlights and taillights might still be visible, and even if there is no clear line of sight, it has been offered that lights from traffic could feasibly find freak reflections, or else just appear at a great distance to someone with an overactive imagination. This theory might be valid for the more recently reported lights, but it does nothing for the older occurrences, such as the two instances in Montana, which were first observed well before the automobile was invented.

More complex theories have emerged. One idea is that the lights are the product of a chemical reaction that occurs when concentrated methane gas from decaying matter is released into the air. Proponents of the methane theory are quick to point out that the majority of earth lights have been sighted on damp, swampy land, where methane is readily found. This theory is interesting enough, but it says nothing for the two occurrences in Montana, which were both reported in arid environments. Other pseudo-scientific explanations have emerged: ball lightning; bioluminescent spore clouds from local vegetation; electric currents generated from tectonic strains; even owls with glowing coats.

Although it is likely that most people will choose to put their faith in these admirably balanced theories, there are others who, perhaps on aesthetic principles alone, will prefer the narrative color of the old folktales. Methane gas or the angry spirits of two dead men wrestling in eternal conflict over the circumstances of their deaths? Fairies taking wing with torches or tectonic strain? Ancient Celtic folktales or modern reason? Perhaps readers would be surprised at the answers that many among us would give to these questions.

The Demons and Spirits on Montana's Highways

It is no secret to anyone with even a passing familiarity with the country's folklore: America's highways are haunted. All across the nation, there are stories of apparitions on lonely stretches of road, appearing at night in the headlights of startled motorists. More often than not, these visions are distraught hitchhikers, usually teenagers and usually female, who are stranded and need assistance of some kind. Often, there has been an accident, but the visibly distressed passengers are rarely able to articulate the details, only wishing to get on to their destinations, which varies from being a town's hospital or police station or to a specified home or address.

Most of the young passengers will never make it to their destination, vanishing instantly from the backseat at some point along the way. Those who do make it to their destinations always end up leaving something they own in the backseat, which the driver finds the next day. When the motorist drives back to return it, he or she learns that the passenger had died in a car accident some time ago, usually at the same place where they were picked up the night before. These patterns are just about universally consistent in these phantom hitchhiker accounts. The stories differ only in the details: a teenager in a bloodstained prom dressed by the side of a highway in the hills of Arkansas, or a stunningly beautiful woman in white down the road from a cemetery on the outskirts of Chicago. But these are only the details. The outcome is always the same—a vanishing passenger and a motorist's chilling realization.

Not every restless roadside spirit is trying to catch a ride. Actually, phantom hitchhikers might be considered one of the more pleasant paranormal encounters that one might have on highways across the nation. Other apparitions have a habit of appearing out of nowhere on the shoulders of innumerable highways, either to leap in front of speeding vehicles, chase them down, or else just plain scare the life out of the drivers. There are reports of hellhounds, headless horsemen, flaming sedans and speeding rigs, or else suicidal phantoms perpetually throwing themselves at horror-struck motorists. There is apparently no shortage of sinister phantoms across the country all too ready to make life miserable for the unlucky travelers they come across.

One of Montana's more famous roadside spirits is said to haunt the McDonald Pass on Highway 12, which enters into Helena. It is on an especially narrow stretch of the alpine road where she comes into sight—always at night, always in a state of frightful panic. She steps from a phone booth at the side of the highway, distraught and waving wildly for the approaching vehicle to stop. The terror on her face is as startling as is her youth; she looked like a young girl in her mid-teens, standing out there on the highway in the middle of the night.

Concerned drivers stop and crane their necks to get a better look. The young girl's sobs are loud and uncontrollable, and she's barely able to get the words out between them. But when she does, the words are always the same. "I have to get home. My father's worried to death about me. I have to get home."

Immediately cowed by the terror in the girl's voice, motorists never think twice about the matter. Urgently, they tell the girl to get into the car. She is still sobbing in the back of the car, curled tightly in the dark, a little more than a shadow in the rearview mirror. Asked where her father lives, she manages to stutter out the address while weeping—it is a house on Breckenridge in Helena. She does not respond to any other questions.

Continuing on to Helena, the uneasy silence in the car is broken occasionally by her muffled sobs from the back-seat, and any attempt by the driver to get more information is left unanswered, which makes for the awkward drive into town, until the car pulls up onto the dim light of Breckenridge and then in front of her father's house. If the girl's father is expecting her or worried about her absence, there is no indication. The lights are out. The door is shut.

Even before the car has come to full stop, the girl is out on the driveway, slamming the car door shut before the driver is able to say a single word to her. She runs across the yard, disappearing into the darkness along the side of the house—and so ends the encounter with the girl on McDonald Pass.

Only upon returning home does the motorist discover that the girl has left her sweater behind on his backseat—torn and filthy and smudged with blood. Resolved to return it, the motorist drives back to the house the next day, where he makes the most startling discovery. The girl's father answers the door, and when he sees the sweater in the passenger's hand, he lets out a long, exasperated sigh. It is all too evident that the arrival of this stranger with the bloody sweater is hardly a surprise.

The man with the sweater begins to explain, but he is quickly interrupted. "That sweater belongs to my daughter," says the weary man at the door, not bothering to wait for confirmation before he continues. "And you saw her last night. She was out on the highway, on McDonald Pass. She waved you down."

If the father does not notice the man at his door nodding, it is because he is looking straight right through him. For years now, he has greeted several such men at his door, standing there with the same concerned look and the same bloodstained sweater in their hands. "She got into your car and gave you this address. She told you that she had to get home. That I'd be worried sick about her."

The man at the door is fully aware, now, that something is very wrong. He asks, "Is she okay?"

"No, she is not okay," the girl's father responds. "She's been dead for years now. Died in a car accident on McDonald Pass."

The man at the door is dumbstruck. "That doesn't make any sense."

"No, it doesn't," the father says. "Doesn't stop it from happening, though. She's been making the same trip for years now. Pretty well every year, on the night of the accident. I'll take this sweater and put it in her closet, but it'll be gone by tomorrow morning, and it's a safe bet that next year some other fella' driving over McDonald Pass will end up bringing it back again." The man at the door mumbles something when the father thanks him for bothering, and he stands there in shock, even after the father steps back and shuts the door behind him.

This is probably the most popular version of the story of the girl at McDonald Pass. In other versions, the father is delirious with grief when the man appears with the sweater on the dead girl's birthday, instead of the anniversary of the fatal car accident.

The Helena girl is not the only spirit purported to be lurking along Montana's roadsides. Another often repeated tale has a high school student from Conrad appearing on the road about halfway between his hometown and the town of Valier in Pondera County. The story goes that a young man from Conrad had a girlfriend who lived in Valier and so ended up spending a good deal of time on the country road that connected the two towns.

The Conrad student was also a football player, and one fall evening, after practice, he decided to drive to Valier hoping to make a quick visit. As it turned out, it was too much to hope for that night. At some point along the journey, he blew one of his tires and had to pull over to the side of the road. The problem, however, was that there was barely a side of the road to pull over onto. It was a narrow country highway, about a lane and a half, both ways, with next to no shoulder fronting the endless sprawl of wheat fields on either side.

He eased his car to a stop on a long curve in the road, parking his vehicle tightly against the tall wheat fields to his right. He went as far into the wheat as he was able; the stalks were bent over the hood and against the passenger door, but his car was still on the inside lane. There were safer places where one might change a tire, but the young man didn't have any choice in the matter. Flicking on his hazard lights, he got out of his car, pulled the spare tire and tools out of his trunk and placed the jack under the car and began to lift.

There is no telling if he saw the oncoming vehicle before it hit him. The car was moving fast. By the time the driver was able to react to the blinking taillights in front of him, it was too late. He managed to swerve away from the car, but the same could not be said about the figure squatting by the back tire. The car hit the high school student, killing him instantly.

Thus, the legend of Pondera County's phantom passenger begins. A figure appears without warning in the backseats of motorists on the country road between Conrad and Valier. The reports are generally the same— lone drivers taking the route between the two towns become aware of a sudden drop of temperature in their cars and have the overwhelming sense that they are no longer alone. With a single glance into the rearview mirror, the reflection of a dark silhouette in the backseat confirms their impression.

He only makes such appearances in the darkness of the early evening, and there is a notable dearth of details regarding his appearance. Usually he is described as little more than a "dark shape," and "obviously a young man," while others recall details like dark mussed hair and pale skin, all just faintly visible in the dark. There is little variation in what happens next, however.

"It's cold," he says, and his voice is always the same— strained, high-pitched, on the verge of tears. The absolute misery takes nothing away from the horror of the moment. It is, at this point, when the drivers swerve to the side of the road and stops the car, as if the manifestation in the backseat had forced them to do so.

The figure in the backseat speaks again. "I don't know how long I've been out there, now. Seems like forever. The

thing you miss most is people. Just being around and talking. You mind telling me a bit about what's been going on
out there in the world?"

The car shakes as the wheels go over onto the rough
ground past the edge of the road. It is, perhaps, under-
standable that motorists are rarely in the mood for conversation, and their responses tend to be limited to
shocked exclamations. There is the sudden stop, the move
for the door handle, the look over the shoulder and then
the sudden bewilderment when they discover there is no
longer anyone in the backseat. The driver is alone in an
idling car, surrounded by Pondera wheat fields.

This common conclusion ends the phantom passenger
encounter. Whether it is owing to the shocked reactions of
the motorists or a natural skittishness on the part of the
spirit, there has never been any communication past
the phantom's distressed opening words. Brief as the
encounters are, they have been reported frequently enough
to cast the ghostly passenger into the region's folklore.
For years now, the narrow road between Conrad and Valier
has been considered one of the nation's many haunted
thoroughfares.

Disturbing as it surely must be to have an apparition in
the backseat of one's car, the spirit said to haunt the road
around Black Horse Lake near Great Falls tends to be a bit
more traumatizing to the motorists he has come across.
This spirit's most common manifestation is as a man in
denim overalls, standing in the middle of the road in a
wide-legged stance, his arms stretched above his head, as
though he might be trying to wave a car down. In these
instances, descriptions of physical characteristics are
always limited to general observations—tall, broad

shouldered, dressed in denim. That is all startled drivers are able to absorb, for he always appears too suddenly, too close, and eyewitnesses are never able to do a thing about it. Whether attempting to swerve out of the way or slam the breaks, their efforts are always in vain. Without exception, an instant after the denim-clad man's appearance, there is a car running through him.

The first reaction is certainly justified terror. Then the questions begin. Those who are confident in their senses ask, where did the man come from? Where did he go? Was he dead? Why was there not even a bump, not even a nudge, of impact? And then there are those who are not so sure of their faculties: did what appeared to have just happened actually happen?

Yet in all the years that startled motorists have been asking these questions, no one has reappeared out of the darkness to answer them. Are motorists just overcome with relief when they don't discover a body sprawled on the road or see any sign of collision on their vehicles? Or does the mystery of the completely abandoned highway awaken a new terror? Either way, there have been many drivers who have concluded their journeys along Black Horse Lake in fear and confusion, wrestling with the memory of the big, denim-clad man who appeared suddenly before their vehicles.

And yet not all run-ins with the Black Horse Lake apparition have been identical. Some drivers have had much closer encounters. The man in denim does not always appear in front of cars. Sometimes, it is said, he appears upon them. In these instances, he does not appear standing in the middle of the road, but rather sprawled

Apparitions have a habit of appearing out of nowhere on Montana's highways.

atop the hood of whatever car, clinging to the moving automobile, with his face pressed against the hood.

Eyewitnesses to these encounters are able to recall finer points about this apparition. He is described as a big Native American man in denim, with long black hair tied up in a red bandana. He looks as distressed as one might expect of a man clinging to the hood of a speeding car, straining to hold on with his mouth clenched tight. Shocked motorists are rarely given an opportunity to react to this bizarre manifestation, however, for the apparition remains for next to no time at all. He blinks out of sight as quickly as he came, leaving gaping eyewitnesses wondering whether or not to trust their senses.

Unlike the phantom passenger of Pondera County and the distraught hitchhiker of McDonald Pass, there is no account of the Black Horse Lake man's provenance. His ongoing manifestations come with nothing that even remotely resembles an explanation. All that can be said about him is that he is there, and people have seen him, but why he appears is anyone's guess.

Still, by far the strangest tale to emerge from Montana's highways is that of the phantom claimant, as related by C.W. Dolson in the spring 1985 issue of *Montana Magazine*. In his article, "Old One-Eye and Other Lost Souls," Dolson recounts the folktale, in which generous individuals driving at night pull over for a hitchhiker on the side of a secluded highway. He is a bizarre looking man, his practically lipless mouth set into a grim expression, with unsettling eyes that shine with chilling light. Even stranger is his outfit—a perfectly cut black suit jacket over a scarlet vest and spotless white dress shirt. A necktie is knotted perfectly around his neck, and his long pointed shoes are buffed to an oily sheen.

He steps into the automobiles of immediately apprehensive drivers in silence, and he refuses to answer any questions, except when he is asked where he is going, or else what he is doing out there, standing on a deserted road in the middle of the night. And when he speaks, motorists become fully aware that there is something very wrong with their passenger. His voice rolls through the confines of the car—a deep, rumbling timber from lips that barely move at all. "I've come out here to check the borders of my claim," he says. "I best figure what is mine and what is not, before I have to return to my place of business and the routines of banishment, of exile."

His cryptic response might not make a whit of sense to the man or woman in the driver's seat, but the hitchhiker never bothers to clarify. A leaden silence falls over the car again, until they reach the passenger's destination, which he indicates with a spine-tingling shout. "This is the spot, damn you! Stop this thing now!"

The car screeches to a stop in the middle of nowhere and the man verily leaps from the backseat, disappearing into the pitch-black countryside with hideous cackles and unearthly shrieks. Motorists might take a minute or two to regain their composure, but they are never able to make it away before the hitchhiker makes a final appearance. And what an appearance it is.

Tearing out of the darkness at an impossible speed, the hitchhiker has a stoic expression that is transformed into a viciously gleeful one. His cold eyes turn deep red. But it is not until he passes before the headlights that the full extent of the horror is revealed, for in place of his pointed, black shoes are cloven hooves, red and glistening. After shooting the driver a lurid grin, he leaps high into the night sky and vanishes without a trace, either landing far beyond the horizon, or never landing at all.

5
Mysterious Montana

The Spirits of Carroll College

It is said that the blood is still there, splattered across the old sink, with stains running down the sides and splotches on the floor. On some days, the stains are barely visible, having faded over the years, so for those who are unfamiliar with the story, they would hardly notice the discoloration. On other days, however, the stains are gleaming red, a glistening crimson splash of freshly spilt blood in the low light of the fourth floor bathroom in St. Charles Hall. And yet this blood did not fall from a recent wound—for legend tells us the perpetually bleeding sink has been this way for over 40 years, ever since a young Carroll College student fell to his senseless demise.

Probably the school's most well-known urban legend, the story of the tragic accident in St. Charles Hall is short on specifics. When did the alleged death occur? Sometime in the early 1960s. Who was the young man who met his end on the edge of the bathroom sink? Name unknown. What, at least, was his focus of study at the college? Again, not known.

What is known is that he spent the last night of his life touring Helena's bars, swilling enough booze so that he was good and drunk by the time he returned to his dormitory. He climbed the stairs to the fourth floor, walked into the bathroom and to the sink. He could not have been walking too steadily all this time, for he was unable to stand in place in front of the sink long enough to wash.

There would have been an instant commotion when he was discovered later that morning—he was found lying face down on the floor with an ugly gash across his head;

his blood was splattered on the sink and across the floor. His reveling was well known, and it did not take anyone long to make the conclusion. Drunk, he fell hard against the sink, cracking his head on the edge without a sound on the bathroom floor, he died with a cerebral hemorrhage filling his skull with blood, while his classmates slept in the rooms down the hall. Of course, the event would not have become an urban legend if that had been the end of it.

The bathroom was quickly barred from the students after the discovery. Faculty and police were conferred to determine the cause and the body was been taken away, amid the shocked residents in the dormitory. Then the maintenance people were called in for the unpleasant duty of cleaning the mess—mops, sponges, bleach on the floor and sink— to erase all the remnants of the senseless death. The stories began circulating soon after that.

There is no way of knowing how it started. Some accounts tell us it was an early morning maintenance man, others say that it was a lone student stumbling into the bathroom late at night. Whatever the case, student and maintenance man reportedly saw the same thing. Blood, everywhere, was splattered fresh across the sink, down the sides, onto the floor. It was the same sink where the student had fallen days ago, and the blood looked like it was still wet, so even the incredulous witness would have thought that a similar tragedy had occurred—if only there had been a body.

But there was no body. And what was first thought to be blood simply could not be. The substance gleamed like bright, fresh blood, but it would not wash off. Also, blood does not remain red once dried, so it was concluded that someone with a morbid and thoroughly demented sense of humor had obviously decided to splash red paint around the sink the student had died upon.

No one laughed, but a few people were certainly puzzled when the alleged paint did not come off, even under the focused effort of the custodians. Concentrated elbow grease and buckets of paint remover accomplished nothing. They tried every solvent in the maintenance room but nothing worked. As hard as they scrubbed, the crimson stains did not wash away. Paint could not stand up against this scouring, so there was obviously something else going on—something that aroused the strangest speculation.

It did not help matters that the vivid splash of red remained for the next few days, so practically every student in St. Charles Hall got to look at the blood that would not wash away. The most popular explanation was, of course, the obvious—it had something to with the recent death of their fellow student. Blood appeared on the same sink where he died. Moreover, the blood did not wash off, no matter how hard they tried.

Rational explanations were abandoned and supernatural ones abounded: it was a ghostly expression of the student's grief at his untimely demise; it was some kind of message from beyond the grave that all was not as it appeared—that some guilty party had gotten away with murder. Or perhaps it was a psychic manifestation brought on by the grief of his friends and family. Whatever it was, it had turned St. Charles' fourth-floor bathroom into a hot topic on campus, as students crowded in to take a look at the bloody sink.

And then it was gone. No one saw it vanish. It was simply there one day, then gone the next. One morning, the bright red smear was replaced by a barely visible orange stain upon the sink and floor. Questions were asked, but no one claimed responsibility for the clean-up job. The maintenance staff had nothing to say. The student body was as mystified as anyone else, and because the bathroom in St. Charles became even more popular, the administration soon decided it would be best to shut it down.

The fourth-floor bathroom was blocked off, but the matter of the bloodstain did not go away. Curious students still found ways to get in and take a look, and the accounts of what they saw there only added to the growing legend of Carroll College's fourth floor. Some swore the stains they saw were as red and vivid as fresh blood, while others claimed all that was there was a faint, nearly invisible brownish smudge.

The varying reports added more to the mystery. If one took all the eyewitness accounts at face value, the inevitable questions arose. Why was the bloodstain fading and reappearing? What was causing this to happen? As might be expected, a number of the responses tended to be sensational. Indeed, there was no shortage of students at the college who did not hesitate at embracing supernatural supposition. What else could it be? *Of course* it was some spiritual remnant of the unfortunate student who had lost his life so pointlessly. *Of course* his ghost was haunting the fourth floor.

Incredible as it seemed, the theory seemed to gain credence as the years passed. Succeeding generations of students continued to make the trip up to the fourth floor; the blood on the sink continued to be spotted in varying degrees of coloration. Some even spoke of seeing a figure standing before that very same sink, an apparition of a young man, transparent and shimmering, looking down at the vivid splotches of red before vanishing away in a blink. Eventually, there were myriad other purported phenomena in the bathroom to go with the red stain and the apparition: disembodied footsteps, sudden plummeting temperature, a low groaning sound.

But the supposed spirit in the bathroom was not universally accepted as truth. The maintenance staff with regular access to the room insisted that nothing out of the ordinary was occurring in the bathroom. They denied ever seeing an apparition or hearing footsteps or groaning sounds, and claimed that there was nothing exceptional about the stain either; it was a faded, barely visible smear that could have been anything. Moreover, the official reason for why the bathroom had been blocked off had nothing to do with a dead student and a perpetually bleeding sink. The old bathroom simply was in need of renovations that the school was not currently able to afford. Everyone knew (didn't they?) that there was no such thing as ghosts.

And yet whispers about the spirit in the bathroom persisted. Apparently, maintenance was not entirely unified on the matter. Other stories emerged about how the senior janitors would only let new employees in on what was going on in the bathroom after they had worked there for a certain number of months. For some members of the custodial staff, the opportunity to look in on the purportedly haunted bathroom was something of a rite of passage—an initiation into the great mystery of St. Charles Hall. Or so the story went. Some, it was said, were profoundly moved by what they saw in the closed down bathroom. Other custodians went on record as being decidedly underwhelmed about the bathroom, stating that the only

Succeeding generations of students continued to check out the fourth-floor bathroom to see the infamous sink.

thing they saw was a lightly stained sink, while others claimed that on some days the stain was bright red. As much as it was contested over the years, the tale of the bloody sink persisted as one of Carroll College's favorite legends. But it was not the only one.

Indeed, it is said that St. Charles Hall has a number of restless spirits residing within. And while there is no short supply of people who are skeptical about the bleeding sink, many who have spent any time in the dormitory will concede that all is not as it should be in the Carroll College residence. Countless testimonials have emerged over the years with students waking in the middle of the night to the sound of hard footfalls treading across their room, though there was no one visible. A vague apparition has been repeatedly spotted on certain Sunday mornings.

Another popular story has another student jumping to his death from the window at the top of the north stairwell. This purported suicide is the most popular explanation for the wailing sounds that are occasionally heard from the top of the stairwell. A number of students have also claimed to hear the sound of someone shouting and falling from the top floor. Others have claimed to see a falling figure flash by their windows. And yet every one of those alarmed eyewitnesses who poked their heads out their windows to look down for a plummeting peer are always left doubting their own eyes—for there is no one there.

St. Charles Hall is not the only haunted building at Carroll College. While St. Albert's Hall is not nearly as packed with ghostly legends, there is one that is at least as famous as the blood-stained sink. Like the student who died in St. Charles' bathroom, the name of the nun who lost her life on the top floor of St. Albert's Hall has been forgotten. The only information that has survived in the legend was that she had been a resident during the college's early years and she died in her quarters after falling gravely ill with the flu—and ever since then, things have not been the same.

It is impossible to say how many students have had run-ins with St. Albert's phantom, but the accounts have persisted over several decades. The solitary ghost appears before startled students in the halls or else she is heard late at night with her cane tapping on the floor, as she makes her rounds up and down each floor. Some students who were stressed with the demands of their classes claimed to have encountered her in their rooms, experiencing what is usually described as a "presence" arriving with a wave of inexplicable calm and content. They claim that after one of these encounters they suddenly acquire a sense of perspective, where the stack of exams and assignments seem manageable in the grand scheme of things. This gift of peace is what the ghostly nun is famous for, and students who have received it have always been grateful.

However, she has left some residents more rattled than inspired. Certainly, it is easy to imagine how the sight of a black-clad nun standing at the end of the hallway still and silent for several seconds before vanishing out of sight would be unsettling. While some took comfort from the sound of the late-night footfalls in the hallway, others were unnerved by it. Not all students were soothed by the idea of living under the watchful and protective eye of a dead nun.

Apparently, she was more protective of some students than others. For awhile she seemed content to stomp through the hallways, but there were times when she entered certain dorm rooms. It always occurred in the same way: the sound of footsteps stop before a door, the door knob turns and the footsteps continue into the room. She was never visible to the startled students within, but her footfalls took her straight into the room and across the floor to the window. For a few moments, there was silence, until the footfalls strode back across the room, through the door and then back out onto hallway, where the ghostly sister continued her solitary vigil.

Today, St. Albert's Hall is no longer a dorm, but footsteps can still be heard throughout the building. If you ever visit or attend an event at the hall, be sure to keep your senses alerted for any unusual sights or sounds.

Ghost of a Memory

"My father moved the family to Great Falls when I was a kid," says our next eyewitness who goes by the pseudonym "Andrew" for this story. "It was a big old house, I know that for sure, but we only lived there for three years before moving back east, so my recollection of the place and most the stuff that went on there is definitely hazy, to say the least." Still, Andrew goes on to say there is one thing about those distant three years that he claims to remember quite clearly. "I called him Mr. Ditters. When I think about it, I've got no idea what made me think he was a mister instead of a missus. As for 'Ditters,' who knows where that came from."

Andrew's mother asked herself the same question. "At first, I'm pretty sure her attitude was, 'Isn't that cute, my boy's got an imaginary friend.' I guess it isn't such a strange thing, a kid dreaming up an imaginary friend after moving to a new place. The thing was, for those first two years and a bit, she never considered the possibility that there actually was a Mr. Ditters. Not once."

Andrew acknowledges that one can hardly blame his mother for her skepticism. "Some of the things I was throwing out there were pretty spectacular," he says. "I'm pretty sure it started off with Ditters showing up by the swing set in the backyard. That's my first memory of him, just standing there in that dark brown suit he always had on, with the gray shirt and beat-up black leather shoes. It's pretty amazing to me how clear those shoes are in my mind. It's been over 30 years ago now, and I can still picture how scuffed the toes were. His laces were all frayed, too, and the left shoe was cracking open along the side."

As Andrew recalls, the dilapidated state of his visitor's footwear made quite the impression. "Those years are hazy," he says, "but I've got this vague memory of a first conversation, where I was laughing at those shoes and asking him why he was still wearing them if they were so banged up, and then he said something about how he couldn't get any shoes that fit."

After that first exchange, Andrew's mother found herself constantly retrieving her husband's shoes from the backyard. "Yeah, I made sure that Ditters got his pick from a bunch of Dad's shoes, whenever he showed up," Andrew says and laughs. "I remember how it started to really annoy my mom. She thought it was funny at first, but it definitely became an issue after a while. There's the time she still talks about, when she looked out into the backyard during a rainstorm, and saw every one of my dad's shoes out there, getting soaked. I'm sure the whole thing wouldn't have been such a problem if I had taken the effort to bring the shoes back in after Ditters was done with them."

But did Andrew's visitor actually try on all of his father's shoes? "Far as I know, he never tried any of those shoes on. On top of it, I don't remember him even once moving away from that swing set. He didn't say too much, either. Most the time, he usually just stood there and watched me muck around in the backyard."

Not all children would be so amenable to having a strange man appearing out of nowhere to gawk in silence. "I know it sounds dodgy," Andrew says, "but you've got to realize two things. One: I pointed him out more than once to my mother, who always reacted like it was just such a cute thing. Two: it was totally obvious, and I mean even to a five-year-old kid, that there wasn't a single harmful bone in Mr. Ditters' body." Indeed, of all the things that he is able to recollect about his mysterious visitor, it is the trait that stands out the most in Andrew's mind. "That's the thing about Ditters," he says. "He was just such a damn nice guy, like the granddad I never had, I guess. Right away, I knew I had nothing to worry about."

Andrew continues. "But that wasn't all. I was only five, but I understood that Ditters wasn't like anybody else I knew. He watched me play all afternoon without saying a word. I also knew it was pretty damn far from normal for a grown-up to show up in your bedroom after your parents turned off the lights and closed the door. Definitely, I was sure that was strange."

Andrew figures that Ditters began making his nocturnal visits several weeks or months after his first appearance in the backyard. "I can say for sure that we moved to Great Falls right after the end of that school year, and the weather was still nice enough for me to sleep with the window open when he started showing up in my room. So he didn't take too long to get comfortable."

Not that he was reclining on an ottoman and cracking jokes. According to Andrew, Mr. Ditters was just as stiff and reticent during these late-night visits as he was in the daytime. "Those evening visits happened on and off for years," he says, "and it was *exactly* the same every time. He would come by maybe 10 or 15 minutes after my mom shut the door. He would appear out of the darkness, all of a sudden, always standing by my window looking over the backyard. I'd blink once and there he was. Standing there."

Incredibly, young Andrew was just as tolerant of these visits as he was of the ones under the sun. "Even though Ditters never said a word all those times in the backyard, by the time he started showing up at night, I've got to say that I was okay having him around—just fine," Andrew says. "It wasn't as *off* as it might sound now. A lot of people for sure would just assume that it was a creepy sinister thing, but all my memories of Ditters are positive ones. I know how nuts it sounds now, but he was just this kind, old guy who was watching over me."

As it turned out, the most important adult in Andrew's life was not nearly as accepting of Mr. Ditters' presence. "When my mother finally clued into the fact that there was something strange going on with me, she freaked right out," Andrew says.

"I found out later that she and my father were going through a rough patch then. The line they fed me was that Dad was doing a lot of traveling with his work, but years later it came out that they were having serious problems and were practically separated. I was eight years old by then, old enough to notice that something was up with my mother. She went through this phase where she didn't sleep at all. She got this habit of drinking warm milk in the middle of the night. I would hear her in the hall a few times and go down to the kitchen for some milk sometimes, too. She wasn't in the best shape then."

Things only got worse for Andrew's mother when Mr. Ditters entered the picture. It started on one of those nights when Andrew was woken by what he thought was the sound of his mother's footsteps going down to the kitchen. Getting out of bed, he made his way down the kitchen to join her, only to find that the kitchen dark and empty. While he thought it was strange that no one was there, he decided he could use some milk, so he went to the fridge. "I must have been a bit on edge because I got quite the scare when I heard my mom behind me," Andrew recalls. "It's probably one of my clearest childhood memories, the way she looked that night. Her eyes were puffy and red from crying so much, and she was looking at me with this real weird look. It was my mother, but I'd never seen her like that before. It was definitely a scary thing to see. Way scarier than Ditters ever could be."

Andrew asked his mother what was wrong, but it was as though she did not hear him. She simply said, "It's late. What are you doing up?"

"Well, you can't expect an eight-year-old kid to grasp what's really going on in his parents' lives," Andrew says. "I guess things had been adding up in her mind, and I was adding on what amounted to the last straw."

Andrew told his mother he had been woken by footsteps going down the kitchen and suggested that they may have belonged to his long-time silent sentinel. "I just said his name and she completely flipped. She started hollering about how she couldn't believe I still had this 'imaginary friend,' and that it wasn't healthy anymore, at my age. Then she started blaming Ditters on my dad, saying something about how, of course, I was going to create this imaginary father figure when my father was never around. I now think that she was basically channeling all her marital frustrations through me that night, but back then, I had no clue what she was talking about. Plain and simple, she really freaked me out. I think I just ran up to my room and slammed the door. I don't know if she came by to apologize or not." Not for a moment did Andrew's mother pause to consider the possibility that Mr. Ditters might actually exist—an attitude that would change over the course of the next few weeks.

"Things changed between me and my mother after that," Andrew recalls. " You could say that I started getting more than the normal amount of attention from her after that night." Attributing it to his mother's sudden concern that he was not enjoying his childhood, Andrew was hardly thrilled about his mother's intensified focus on him. "All of a sudden I was enrolled in skating lessons and guitar classes. Suddenly it was important for us to spend an hour of the day talking about how we were feeling. She wanted to have these open discussions about the type of man my father was, and that he cared about me but was really busy with his own stuff." At eight years old, Andrew who until very recently had thought everything with his father had been fine, was thoroughly bewildered by his mother's behavior. "It became a lot clearer in retrospect," he says today. "There's no way she could have actually believed I understood the first thing she was talking about. It was about her talking herself through her own issues and insecurities. I think it had next to nothing to do with me." But that was before Mr. Ditters took over.

"It all hit the fan the night my mom came barging into my bedroom," Andrew says. "I remember it was really late at night. She woke me up asking if I'd gone down to the kitchen a few minutes ago; she was obviously scared half to death, and I remember I got scared, too. Fear's funny that way; it can be contagious."

Sitting at the edge of his bed, his mother repeated the urgent question. "When I told her no, that I'd been sleeping all along, she went into classic mom mode, telling me not to panic, even though *she* was the one doing all the panicking. She started going off about how she heard someone going downstairs and how she thought there was somebody in the house."

The way Andrew tells it, he may well have breathed his first indignant sigh at eight years old. "I can't say for sure how she took it when I told her that it was no big deal. I'd seen him in my room before I fell asleep that night, standing by my window as usual. I told my mom that what she heard was Mr. Ditters and not to worry, because I heard him walking around the other night, and that he never did any harm." His mother's response was very different from what it had been the night in the kitchen.

"Don't ask me how, but this time, her kid's mention of the resident ghost calmed her right down. She told me to stay put and flipped on the light in my room. She went through the whole place, turning on every light in the house and checking all the doors and windows." Returning to his bedside after her tour, she asked him about the man who had been his silent companion for the last three years. "More than anything, what I remember most about that night was how *seriously* my mother was taking me. I don't think I'd ever had an adult ever hanging on my words that way. Come to think of it," Andrew says laughing, "it probably hasn't happened again since."

His mother listened to what he had to say, casting a number of uneasy glances at the space by the open window where Andrew claimed Mr. Ditters frequently stood. "It's hard to say for sure because it was such a long time ago, but if I remember right, she calmed down after that," Andrew says. She left the room, but not before going to his window and locking it shut.

After turning every light in the house on and checking all the doors and windows, she asked Andrew about his silent companion.

Andrew's theory on his mother's acceptance of Mr. Ditters hinged on her surrendering to the idea of a presence in her home that was beyond her control. A nice thought, perhaps, but her actions over the subsequent days and weeks did not exactly paint a picture of acquiescence. "The first thing she did was insist that I keep my bedroom window locked. When I told her that it would get way too hot, she moved a fan up into my room. I tried telling her that locking the window wouldn't help because Ditters showed up just the same in the winter when the window was shut." Sure enough, Andrew's friend ended up swinging by for a visit that night, leaving the window open for his mother the next morning.

"One thing I do have to say is that Ditters really got me thinking, the way he left the window open that night," Andrew says. "I wasn't lying to my mother. He showed up in the winter just as much as he did in the summertime, and he never once needed to open the window to be there. It seemed like he did it just to get a rise out of my mother. There was no other reason for it, really."

And did it get the intended rise? According to Andrew, his mother did not react the way he might have expected. "It's funny," he says, "she actually took it all in stride." Telling her son to get ready for his day, she made breakfast and sent him off to school.

Calm as she appeared, when Andrew returned from school that day, he discovered that his mother had been busy. "She moved me into the spare bedroom. She moved everything out—my desks, my books, all my posters. Everything I owned in the world was moved down the hall." Not a big move by any means, but enough to fill an eight-year-old boy with resentment. "I know I was upset about it. Really unhappy," Andrew says. Apparently, so was Mr. Ditters.

"The funny thing about it all is how Ditters and I got along without any fuss for three years or so, but as soon as my mom got involved, everything there got crazy. Those last few months in that place ended up eclipsing all that time when everything was fine. It always bugged me how things with Ditters ended.

"That same night, me and my mom woke up to a banging in the kitchen. It was a loud and repetitive sound, and I was more excited than scared when I heard it from my bed. For me it was like, '*This* is new. What the hell can Ditters be up to down there?'"

Andrew's mother, however, was not as enthusiastic. The fear was plain on her face when Andrew bumped into her in the hallway. The pair ran down into the kitchen to find every cupboard and drawer pulled open, as well as the fridge and freezer doors. The tap was running and the dog food was scattered all over the floor. "I thought it was great that Ditters was standing up to my mom who was being completely unreasonable. But she was nowhere near beat." Promptly cleaning the dog food off the floor and tucking everything away, she calmly told her son to go back up to bed.

Andrew has a theory about how his mother was able to deal with what was going on. "She was definitely scared of Ditters, I'm sure of that, but she was so calm about dealing with him," Andrew says. "Dealing with Ditters got insane, but it was probably a nice change from dealing with my dad. There's a part of me that thinks it must have been a welcome distraction from her marital issues."

Before they settled in for bed the next night, Andrew noted that his mother had tied the drawers, cupboards and fridge shut and moved the dog food out to the garage. "I didn't have a solid grasp of the order of events on the first night," Andrew says. "But tying everything down didn't really accomplish anything. He just moved on to other things."

Other things like strobing the hallway lights, messing around with electric appliances and running the water in the kitchen and the bathroom at all hours. Each new occurrence was a treat for wide-eyed young Andrew, who had not known his phantom friend was capable of such mischief. As for Andrew's mother, she met each occurrence with silent and staunch resolve. "When I think about it now, I'm actually amazed at how my mother dealt with it all. Seriously, if it happened just to me, I'd be losing my mind."

Yet mother and son stayed on, until, that is, Mr. Ditters decided it was time to appear before Andrew's mother. "We were having supper at the kitchen table when I saw him through the screen door. He was standing there in the backyard, where he always did, looking right at us." Andrew did not think to say anything, with Ditters' appearances having long lost their novelty, but he was genuinely surprised when his mother let out a gasp and dropped her fork on the floor.

"That was pretty incredible," Andrew says. "I was the only one who'd seen him for so long, so to have someone else see him was this major event. I was blown away. So was Mom." Perhaps more than blown away, she apparently decided right there at the dinner table that they were leaving. "I was sent over to sleep over at a friend's place that night and only stayed for a few more days before my mother flew us over to Michigan, where we got back together with my father. I've never been back to Great Falls since."

According to Andrew, today, his mother barely acknowledges Mr. Ditters. "It's actually quite incredible," he says. "There's been times where I've tried to bring the whole thing up, and she completely dismisses it. She'll say something about how hard those times were without Dad, and how she prefers to remember the good times. But she won't say *anything* about Ditters. Not a *word*. I really think that she's managed to convince herself that nothing happened. She's in complete denial."

As for his own reflections, for the most part, Andrew has put his early-life encounters with the unknown behind him. "Of course something like that affects a person," he says. "Not every kid ends up finding that his supposed imaginary friend wasn't so imaginary after all." Andrew takes a thoughtful pause before continuing: "Then again, I never let it take me over. I guess I've accepted that this was something that happened, and I'm not going to dedicate my life chasing down shadows in the hopes that I'll be able to make some sense of it, like some people do. I don't know who Mr. Ditters was, and I accept that I probably never will."

And so Andrew has let Mr. Ditters rest in his memory, not denying his existence outright, but not allowing himself to be possessed by his extraordinary experiences either. Who was Mr. Ditters? Why was he haunting this particular Great Falls home? Why did he appear solely to Andrew and then react so strongly when his mother interfered? Impossible to say—an answer, incidentally, that Andrew claims to be more than happy with.

A Ghostly Murder Mystery

Mary Ann Eckert was on her deathbed when she breathed the confession. "I was the one who did in John Denn," she said, her eyes clear and urgent. "I was the one who fooled him into that damned cellar. When he turned his back on me, I took out my hatchet and hit him a lick. That was the end of him." Mary Ann died on May 3, 1888, shortly after she made her incredible admission, and the unsolved murder of John Denn, who met his end in the cellar of his liquor store nearly 10 years before, was once more the center of Helena's attention.

John Denn was a German-born businessman who was drawn to the United States in the 1849 gold rush. He eventually settled in Helena, where he opened up a lucrative business on Wood Street, selling booze to the town's reliably thirsty inhabitants. Successful as he was, it seems as though he dipped into his wares with a bit too much frequency. When this happened, Denn was always one of the loudest men in the room. One of his favorite topics of conversation was his hatred of banks. He would often holler that he did not trust any of the town's banks with a single dime of his fortune and kept all his money— thousands, he would shout—in a safe in his store. In the 1870s, Helena was not nearly as dangerous as it had been in the preceding decade, but it had not completely forgotten its boomtown origins. It was still filled with ambitious young miners who would do much to possess half the fortune Denn routinely bragged about. No one believed Denn's noisy rants were good for his health.

Late in the evening of October 27, 1879, John Denn was settling down for bed. He had his nightshirt on and was just about to blow out his bedroom candle when there was a sharp rap at his back door. This was not so unusual. Known to sell bottles to townsfolk after hours, Denn was occasionally woken from sleep by someone desperate for a drink. Lit candle in hand, Denn walked down to the door and greeted his late-night visitor, who, sure enough, was in need of a bottle of whiskey. Inviting the individual inside, Denn led his customer down to his cellar, where he stored his casks of rotgut. Grabbing a funnel and a bottle, he reached down to turn the faucet. That was when the caller acted. A blunt weapon was raised and brought down hard on the back of Denn's head, producing a fatal cavity in his skull. Denn collapsed, receiving two more vicious blows over each eye before he was left there to die.

Because he dispensed such a valued service to Helena residents, he was immediately missed when he failed to open his establishment the next morning. It was not yet noon when his corpse was discovered, crumpled before his whiskey cask. The intruder had broken into Denn's much-advertised safe and made away with its contents, with the exception of a hidden tin box that contained almost $7000.

The crime sent a nervous tremor through Helena's townsfolk, who, having seen their fair share of crime and chaos in the 1860s, were not so eager to revisit those days. A $12,000 reward was offered to the person who could bring Denn's murderer to justice, but nothing ever came of it. There were no witnesses, no strong suspects and no charges laid. The whole town buzzed with whispers of recrimination as residents began speculating on possible culprits and concocting all sorts of theories and suspicions. It was not a happy time.

In the end, there was no resolution to the case. While all sorts of speculation abounded, the investigation into Denn's death went nowhere. Helena's law enforcement was not able to get any further than the murder site, which yielded only a bludgeoned corpse, a half-turned whiskey spigot and an emptied safe. Anyone in Helena could have done it. Nevertheless, a slow-burning public suspicion turned to two Helena residents whose names became irreversibly connected to the murder: John Shober and Mary Ann Eckert.

John Shober, a respected member of the community, was one of Helena's top attorneys and a card-carrying constituent of the esteemed Montana Club. Despite his impressive frontier standing, events in the wake of Denn's murder revealed him to have connections with some of the seedier elements in Helena society. One of these elements was Mary Ann Eckert.

Among Helena's earliest citizens, Eckert was one of the typically willful women who came west with the first wave of settlers. She opened a photography studio in 1868 and might have been a respectable resident of the fledgling town, but there were details in her past that made her a topic of conversation among the town's stiff collars. First, there was the question of her early occupation in Helena's mining camp days. Although she had graduated to photography, there were rumors that she had come to Helena as a prostitute, working the saloons and hurdy-gurdy houses until she was able to establish herself. The fact that her house and business were in the most disreputable part of town, and that she made no effort to move, did little to dispel such gossip. Neither did her dubious divorce proceedings, which were never finalized, nor the rumors of a romantic affair she was having with an unidentified man of Helena's elite. When her estate was made public after her death, the controversy was reborn. Her estranged husband was left with one dollar on the nose, while it was revealed that she owned some $25,000 in real estate, most of it concentrated in Helena's red-light district. Her only debt was an unpaid $650 loan from John Shober.

The connection between Shober and Eckert was no great revelation. Both were early arrivals in Helena; they had known one another from the time of the town's early origins. And each of them had associated with John Denn as well. Although the depth of this "association" was never made completely clear, the ensuing weeks after Eckert's deathbed confession, rather than shed light on the still-unsolved murder, only complicated the issue.

After Eckert was buried, Helena's deputy marshal came forward with contradictory statements that the recently deceased woman had made about the crime. Apparently, Eckert had made more than one late-night visit to the deputy's house, where she repeatedly accused Shober of murdering Denn and of making attempts on her life as well. It was true that Eckert was attacked by an unidentified hatchet-wielding assailant some years back, but the deputy did not take Eckert's frantic protestations seriously, assuming them to be the delusional rants of a woman who, for whatever reason, had never been able to put the murder of John Denn behind her.

There was no arguing with the fact that Eckert was never the same after Denn's murder. With her peace of mind shattered, Eckert became full of foreboding portent, which she expressed regularly to friends and acquaintances.

The murder investigation yielded only a bludgeoned corpse, a half-turned whiskey spigot and an emptied safe.

There always seemed to be some uncertain and imminent disaster hovering before her feverish eyes. Suffering from a crippling mental anguish, she became difficult to understand, all the while consistently obsessing about the long-dead Denn. The murdered booze seller was all she seemed able to think about. Roughly a year before her death, a construction crew was putting up a new building on the site of Denn's liquor store. Eckert would stand at the excavation site for hours, the blood drained from her face, staring at the workers with a horrified expression transfixed on her face. A friend, seeing Eckert standing there in such a state, wearily asked what she was doing in the middle of the street.

She turned to the man with a haunted look and said, "I am watching that accursed spot."

Although she was obviously plagued by Denn's murder and seemed to be involved in one way or another, Eckert was never able to provide reliable and consistent information on the crime. There were her repeated visits to the deputy marshal, during which she indicted Shober for the crime, but then she also reportedly confessed to her nurse that she had gotten in a quarrel with Shober and had been trying to frame the attorney for some time. And while some people might have been tempted to take her final admission to heart, she stated that she had murdered Denn with a hatchet, yet forensic evidence indicated that a hatchet had not been involved.

In the end, a dark cloud of suspicion would forever hang over both Eckert and Shober. Old, forgotten stories re-emerged in the wake of Eckert's death. There were the rumors of her affair with a powerful local man. A story printed in the newspaper weeks after Denn's murder resurfaced. In it, Shober was reported heading to Bozeman for a business meeting, happier than any of his associates had ever seen him. His mood was not enough to put him away, or even put him up on trail, but it was more than enough to get chins wagging.

Denn, a sworn bachelor, was well known for lending money to the girls in the red-light district. Upon Eckert's death, it was revealed she owed money to Shober. At one time, was there some conflict between Denn and Shober for Eckert's attention? Some townsfolk believed so. The theory revealed the identity of Eckert's mysterious lover, while also explaining Shober's elevated mood when he took his trip to Bozeman. Nevertheless, others refuted the theory, bringing up the fact that it had been Shober who, while investing the crime scene, had found the tin box containing the $7000 in the cellar—the $7000 that whoever killed Denn had missed.

To cap the mystery off, a short time after Eckert died, a man came galloping into Helena and made a straight line for the district attorney's office. There, this man, breathless, wild-eyed and disheveled, insistently stuttered that he knew who killed John Denn. It was his business partner, an unscrupulous man who had long ago confided that he was the murderer who had evaded justice.

When this obviously distressed man was asked why he had decided to come forth with this information now, he began to babble about a terrible vision he endured the night before. Woken from sleep by an ice-cold draft, he sat up to see none other than John Denn standing at the foot of the bed, pale as paper with three bleeding wounds on his forehead. The terrified man could only stare as the apparition spoke: "You know the murderer. Hand him over to justice so that I may sleep in peace." Denn's wounded apparition gave his message and then disappeared, and the poor man in bed wasted no time saddling his horse and heading for Helena. He had half lost his mind by the time he arrived in town.

The attorney sent the authorities after this man's business partner, but the newly accused man had made his getaway before the law could reach him. Even then, however, suspicion was not entirely lifted from Shober, as the self-proclaimed witness to Denn's ghost was shortly after declared insane and locked up in an asylum.

In the end, Denn's murder went unpunished. At least, officially unpunished, for no one can say for certain if any off-the-record vindication took place, as is so often the case where there is a murder. Either way, if the madman who rode into the district attorney's office really did see what he claimed to have seen, then the killer never was brought to justice, and Denn's spirit never found peace.

Some people say that Denn still wanders the earth around his old business to this day. It is said that he appears on nights when a full moon is shining, a lone figure in anachronistic frontier dress, wandering the area between the old Federal Building and the Lewis and Clark Library. Wood Street once ran through the grassy stretch between the two buildings. Denn, the shadowy, silent phantom, is the only one with answers to the long-unsolved mystery. He moves slowly over the site where his cellar is buried, pale and bleeding, with his skull perforated in three places and a ghastly and inexplicable smile on his face.

The End